Pioneering in Montana

CARROL OR ROCKY POINT, MONTANA, IN 1881

This was a rendezvous of horse thieves and cattle rustlers, and here some of them were hanged by vigilantes

From a photograph by F. J. Haynes of St. Paul

PIONEERING IN MONTANA
The Making of a State, 1864–1887

By
Granville Stuart

Edited by
Paul C. Phillips

University of Nebraska Press
Lincoln and London

Publishers on the Plains

UNP

Copyright, 1925, by The Arthur H. Clark Company

Originally published under the title *Forty Years on the Frontier as seen in the Journals and Reminiscences of Granville Stuart, Gold-Miner, Trader, Merchant, Rancher and Politician*, Volume II.

First Bison Book printing: 1977

Most recent printing indicated by the first digit below:
2   3   4   5   6   7   8   9   10

Library of Congress Cataloging in Publication Data

Stuart, Granville, 1834–1918.
   Pioneering in Montana.

   Reprint of v. 2 of Forty years on the frontier published by A. H. Clark, Cleveland, which was issued as no. 2 of Early western journals.
   Includes index.
   1. Frontier and pioneer life—Montana.
2. Ranch life—Montana.   3. Indians of North America—Montana.   4. Pioneers—Montana—Biography.
5. Ranchers—Montana—Biography.   6. Montana—Biography.   7. Stuart, Granville, 1834–1918.
I.   Title.   II.   Series: Early western journals; no. 2.
F731.S912   1977b   978.6'02'0924   [B]   77–7651
ISBN 0–8032–0933–9
ISBN 0–8032–5870–4 pbk.

Manufactured in the United States of America

Edition Note

PIONEERING IN MONTANA: THE MAKING OF A STATE, 1864–1887, originally was published as Volume II of Stuart's *Forty Years on the Frontier*, edited by Paul C. Phillips. The first volume, published by the University of Nebraska Press under the title PROSPECTING FOR GOLD: FROM DOGTOWN TO VIRGINIA CITY, 1852–1864, includes an introduction by the editor, a preface, and twelve chapters: "Early Life"; "Overland to California"; "Experiences in California"; "The Rogue River War"; "From California to Montana"; "The Discovery of Gold"; "Trading Experiences"; "Settlement of Deer Lodge Valley"; "Life in Early Montana"; "Gold Mining in Deer Lodge Valley"; "Bannack and Pike's Peak"; and "Virginia City." Since PIONEERING IN MONTANA is a continuation, the annotation begins with footnote 93 and it carries the index for both volumes.

Contents

Illustrations

First Years of Montana Territory[93]

In February, 1864, my brother James started with a second expedition to the Yellowstone. A place on the Gallatin river about twenty-five miles below Gallatin City was selected as the place of rendezvous. A company of seventy-five joined him and on February 27, they started on their expedition.

This was a cold late spring, snow lay on the ground so that they could not get up into the mountains to prospect. They found Lieutenant Menadier's camp on the Stinking river fork of the Big Horn, where he reported his party had found gold in paying quantities in 1858. They prospected thoroughly, but could not find more than a color. The formation was sandstone and it is certain that Lieutenant Menadier was duped by some of his men for there never was gold there or near there.

At this place the entire party split up. James decided to return to Deer Lodge and about twenty-five men accompanied him. The others scattered about over the country; some intending to prospect more thoroughly when the snow was gone. On this trip they did not see either Sioux or Crow Indians. James and his following reached Virginia City on the eighteenth of May. The rest of the party returned during July and August: they went to the Sweetwater river and then split up into small parties and straggled back,

---

93 Here Mr. Stuart has two chapters; one called *The Knights of the Road,* the other *The Vigilantes.* Both closely parallel Langford, *opus citra,* and are omitted. – Ed.

some by the Emigrant road, and some through the mountains. None of them succeeded in finding any diggings that would pay.

Soon after James left them two men went out hunting; a sudden snow storm came up and lasted three days. They became bewildered and separated; one finally turned and tried to overtake those who were returning with James, but fell in with a small camp of Crow Indians on the Rosebud (a branch of the Yellowstone) who robbed him of all he had and compelled him to stay with them for a couple of weeks. At the end of that time he persuaded them to go with him to the Gallatin valley; telling them that they could get a good trade with the white people there. After much persuasion the Indians consented to go. The Crows were always a hard lot of Indians to trade with and they did not succeed in making any trade, but Indian Dick by this ruse succeeded in getting back among his friends and took one of their best horses to reimburse himself for the things they had robbed him of. This, however, did not profit him much for the horse soon took sick and died, and thereupon he came to me and borrowed twenty dollars to buy himself some clothes as he was almost naked. Which twenty dollars he still owes in this year 1916.

The other man's body was found during the summer of 1865, lying in the willows on the Stinking river near where he left the party when he started hunting on that ill-fated morning. He had been shot, as was supposed by Indians and had run into the brush and died there. The Indians had not dared to follow him, as his gun, clothes, etc., were all there, but his horse was found among the Crows a year later.

So ended my brother's second Yellowstone expedi-

tion. These two expeditions had cost us two thousand
dollars in money and loss of much valuable time and
many precious lives. It was our last attempt to open
up the Yellowstone country.

Jim Bridger and John Jacobs made a road from the
Red Buttes on North Platte to Virginia City via Wind-
river, Stinking river, Pryors fork, Clarks fork and the
Yellowstone river and a large number of wagons came
by that route.[94] Some of them turned and went up the
Yellowstone above the first cañon and prospected for
gold and found some diggings and called the place
Emigrant gulch. First among these miners was my
old friend, D. B. Weaver. There was a grand stampede from Virginia City to Emigrant gulch, but as the
mines there were not extensive most of them returned.[95]

Our partner, W. B. Dance, had been in St. Louis
for some time purchasing goods for the firm. Early in
April he left St. Louis, on the "Welcome" for Fort
Benton. The trip was a tedious one, the water being
very high and the swift current carried much drift
wood and logs that greatly hindered the old side-
wheeler boats then used on the Missouri. There was
no fuel provided for the boats on the upper river and
they were obliged to stop and allow the crew to cut
sufficient cord wood to last until another landing could
be made.

At the mouth of the Yellowstone, Judge Dance got

---

[94] For further account of the Bridger trail see Grace R. Hebard and E. A.
Brininstool, *The Bozeman Trail*, vol. ii, p. 119, n. and index. Jacobs was
connected with Bozeman instead of Bridger. The *Fort Owen Journals* con-
tain probably the earliest description of the Bridger road. – ED.

[95] Mr. D. B. Weaver of Saxton, Pennsylvania was one of the party that
discovered Emigrant gulch. He has written a splendid description of that
event, in the *History of the Yellowstone Valley*, published by the Western
Historical Publishing Co., Spokane, Washington. G. S. Mr. Weaver is still
living in Saxton, Pennsylvania (1924). – ED.

off the steamer to lay off a town site which he called "Oraopolis." While thus engaged the boat pulled out and left him. Securing a horse from Fort Union he started out and tried to overtake the boat, but the horse was a poor traveler and gave out and Dance was obliged to leave him below the mouth of Milk river and proceed on foot. His situation was now desperate: He was without food or blankets, in the midst of a hostile Indian country. After traveling for two days without food, he managed to reach Fort Galpin [96] where he remained until another boat came along and took him on to Fort Benton and later he arrived in Virginia City without further mishap.

Early in June, 1864, we formed a partnership with Frank Worden and opened a store in Deer Lodge and brother James went over there to live; leaving me in the store at Virginia City.

The autumn of 1864 was beautiful and there was no severe weather until about the tenth of December, when a sudden storm came on: the thermometer fell to thirty-seven degrees below zero and a foot of snow fell in the valleys. Chinook winds refused to blow, the first snow lay on the ground and daily storms added to it until there were two feet of snow in the valleys and from five to six feet on the divides.

On September 24, 1864, a party of twenty-five men furnished with the necessary implements, started for the Yellowstone to build boats for a journey east down the river. They were to build twelve boats large enough to accommodate twelve passengers each. One hundred twenty men had signed to go on this trip. The boats were to be completed October first. William

---

[96] Fort Galpin was a small post about fifteen miles west of the mouth of the Milk river. – ED.

Young with a company of ninety-four men left Virginia City late in September on foot, with their luggage hauled in ox wagons.

On their arrival at the boat yard, a point on the Yellowstone near where the town of Livingston now is, they expected to find the boats ready to start but to their surprise and chagrin they found but two boats just begun. Some of the party became disgusted and returned to Virginia City with the ox wagons; but about seventy-five turned in and helped finish the boats which were little better than rafts, and on the seventh day, all being ready, the start was made. The river was low and full of sand bars; in many places the current was swift and the boats unwieldy, they were no sooner off one sand bar than they were caught on another. The provisions were getting low and they were obliged to hunt game for food and the game was scarce along the river at that season of the year. A severe storm came on, nine inches of snow fell and the river filled with mush ice.

The ammunition was getting low and the captain took charge of all on board. Six of the best hunters were selected to do the hunting, no shots were fired only when necessary to get food. The party was on half rations most of the time and suffered severely with the cold.

When twenty miles above Fort Union the boats froze in; the party was obliged to abandon them with most of their luggage and make it to Fort Union on foot. Thirty days had been spent on the Yellowstone, during which time they had suffered everything but death. Twenty-five of the party gave up the trip and remained at Fort Union. Forty-eight kept on to Fort Berthold, there twenty more of the party elected to stay until

spring, and tried to persuade their companions to do
likewise but some were homesick and the desire to meet
their friends and families urged them to go forward.

On December 3 thirty of the party left Berthold on
foot; they were well supplied with ammunition and
good firearms, but little else. The first night out it
begun to snow and continued to do so for three days.
The little army of travelers lost their way and after
wandering about until exhausted they lay down on the
storm-swept plains without fires until the storm abated.
Twenty-three of the party returned to Fort Berthold,
but Young with six companions continued the journey.
The weather had cleared up and the little party was
making good time: no difficulty had been experienced
in getting what game was required.

One evening while camped on the river bottom, preparing their evening meal they were surprised by a
band of Indians who took them prisoners. Three of
the party had been hunting and had deposited their
guns and some ammunition beside a log just outside of
camp, where they had been dressing an antelope. The
Indians marched them all off to their village, some
three miles further down the river. There were about
fifty lodges and three hundred Indians, men, women,
and children. The prisoners were taken to a lodge
near the center of the village and while the Indians
had not shown any disposition to hurt them, still they
were not particularly friendly and had taken possession
of all the firearms in sight and all the blankets. The
prisoners were not bound but they felt certain that they
were so carefully guarded that it would be useless to
try to escape. After all the Indian men in the lodge
had been fed, a squaw brought some roasted buffalo
meat and gave it to the captives. The meat was dry

and hard and without salt, but it was eaten with relish just the same. After eating their meat they were assigned a place in the lodge where they could lay down and sleep. The lodge was warm and comfortable but they were given no robes or blankets to lie upon and were too anxious to learn their ultimate fate to sleep very much.

Early next morning they were awakened by a group of young Indians who drove them out of camp and ordered them to go – pointing down the river. The ground was covered with snow and it was bitter cold, but the captives were glad to escape on any terms.

When they were out of sight, they circled around and made for their camp of the day before and to their great joy found the guns and ammunition and one hunting knife where they had left them. Securing the guns they lost no time in getting out of that neighborhood and traveled forty miles that day. The weather grew colder and a nipping north-east wind chilled them to the bone. Most of the party had frozen their hands and feet and traveling next day was slow and painful and they only made fifteen miles.

Finding a sheltered nook in a deep ravine near a timbered bottom, they made camp. Young and Burton went for wood and carrying it to camp on their shoulders, Burton dropped his end of the log and broke Young's collar bone. The situation had been bad enough but this last calamity made it critical. Burton refused to leave Young, so it was at last decided that they remain in camp while the others pushed on to Fort Rice where they could get a team to send back for the injured man.

That same evening three families of friendly Indians came along and seeing the camp fire paid a call. These

Indians were on their way to Fort Rice. From them they learned that the fort was fifty miles distant. The Indians offered to take the men to the fort. One of the squaws, exercising much ingenuity in fixing up a travois, made the injured man comfortable. Eight miles from Fort Rice they met the team and turned it back. The little company spent two weeks at Fort Rice waiting for Young's recovery and then joined an ox train bound for Sioux City, Iowa. The trip was made in four weeks.

At Sioux City the company divided; Young went by stage to Tella and from there by rail to Tonlon, Stark county, Illinois, by rail.[97] He spent the remainder of the winter in Illinois, but was again in Virginia City, Montana the next summer, having returned by the way of Salt Lake City.

In September, Virginia City was incorporated and we put on regular city airs. There were about ten thousand people in the district and the greater part of them lived in Virginia City.

During the summer of 1864 Stuart and Hauser purchased six silver quartz claims on Rattlesnake creek in Beaverhead county and started development work in them. In addition to looking after the store in Virginia City, I kept the books for the Deer Lodge store and the mining camps and had to attend to getting the goods for the stores freighted from Fort Benton to Deer Lodge and Virginia City.

The new year saw marvelous changes in Montana: from a primeval wilderness, inhabited by a few roving bands of Indians and an occasional trader or trapper, we had emerged into a full fledged territory, with a

---

[97] Young gave the details of this story in a letter from Illinois to Reece Anderson.

population of fourteen thousand eight hundred seventeen souls. Many new and important gold discoveries had been made at Prickley Pear, Last Chance, Silver Bow, and Ophir.[98] Thriving villages had sprung up at all of these places.

The first territorial legislature was in session at Bannack, enacting laws for better government.[99] Emigrants were thronging into all the principal valleys and many fine ranches were being improved. Virginia City was an incorporated town: law now reigned supreme, offenders were promptly arrested and tried by authority of judge and jury. Good public schools were provided wherever six or more children could be assembled. Professor Dimsdale conducted a singing school where lovers of good music met once a week for instructions and practice.

There was also a lyceum where lectures were given by men of undoubted talent and knowledge. Two large and commodious churches were built and crowded congregations listened with reverence and attention to the sermons. Two Sabbath schools were in successful operation. The Reverend Father Giorda, a missionary father, ministered to the spiritual needs of Catholics; celebrating mass each Sunday.

The Montana Historical Society was organized with Wilbur F. Sanders as president, Judge H. L. Hosmer, historian, and Granville Stuart, secretary. There was a strong Masonic lodge in Virginia City and during the summer the organization built a handsome Masonic hall.

---

[98] Last Chance was discovered by John Cowan in 1864 and later became Helena. Prickley Pear and Ophir are near there. Silver Bow is near Butte. – ED.

[99] Montana was organized as a territory from northeastern Idaho, May 26, 1864. – ED.

A daily mail and stage service was in operation between Virginia City, Bannack, and Salt Lake City and a weekly stage from Virginia to other towns in the territory carried mail and passengers. A great number of steamboats made regular trips from St. Louis, Missouri, to Fort Benton and each one was loaded to capacity with freight and passengers.

Early in the spring six dromedaries were brought up from Arizona and it was proposed to start a pack train from Virginia City to Fort Benton. The claim was made that the dromedaries could travel much faster, carry a greater load and that as the Indians were afraid of them, the trains would escape raids from the aborigines. Circulars were distributed about Virginia City advertising exhibitions to take place on the street, where would be demonstrated how a dromedary would carry ten children or one thousand pounds of freight, that they would kneel and raise at the word of command, etc.

An exhibition was given in front of the Gibson House on Idaho street and it was easily shown that the dromedaries could carry ten or more children. Every youngster was on hand for a trial ride. One young lady of sixteen summers perched comfortably on one of the kneeling animals, but when the awkward beast attempted to regain its feet she was wholly unprepared for the sudden dip forward and was pitched head first into the street, but fortunately escaped serious injury. This mishap brought the exhibition to a close and as the strange animals frightened every horse that came in sight of them, causing serious runaways, the owner was ordered to take them out of town.

They were removed to the valley in the neighborhood of Snow Shoe gulch, where they remained for sometime. One day a hunter spied an animal browsing in a clump of willows and taking aim fired, the animal dropped and thinking he had killed an elk, he ran up to secure his game; what was his astonishment to find a camel instead of an elk. Not having heard of the dromedary train, he was much puzzled to know where the animal came from, but was soon enlightened by the appearance of the owner on the scene, who informed him in a very pointed and energetic manner that the camel was his. "Well Mister," replied the Nimrod, "you can have the camel if it is yours." The dromedary train proved a failure and the remaining five animals were taken to Utah and Montana saw them no more.

Early in the year Mr. A. M. Smith arrived in Virginia City with a camera and photographic supplies and opened a gallery over "Con" Orem's saloon. The place was crowded with people every day, all anxious to have likenesses taken to send home. Most of us had a tintype taken and then this enterprising man, Smith, would place it in a little black case lined with red velvet, call it a "daugerrotype" and charge us $5.00 for the same. The photograph gallery was as profitable as a "claim" in the bed of Alder gulch.

There was also a "hair dressing parlor" opened by Thomas White, where one could not only have his hair cut and combed, but could also have it colored, the proprietor even going so far as to guarantee that the shade would be a beautiful glossy black or brown.

The hardest fought prize fight on record was called for January 1, 1865, at Virginia City: between John Condel Orem and Hugh O'Neil for one thousand a side. That date falling on Sunday, Professor Dimsdale appealed to both contestants to change the date to Monday, January 2, to which they cheerfully consented.

The ring was pitched at the lower end of the Leviathan hall, on the north side of Jackson street. Precisely at fifteen minutes past one o'clock Hugh O'Neil shied his sombrero into the ring followed by one hundred ninety pounds of as good bone and sinew as one could expect to look upon. "Con" Orem instantly reciprocated and deposited his castor over the ropes introducing one hundred thirty-eight pounds of as tough humanity as ever crossed the Rocky mountains or any other mountains for that matter. "Con" Orem was thirty years of age, stood five feet six and a half inches and was a model of symmetry, form, wiry and healthy, with a boxer's eye. Scarcely could an improvement be suggested. His training had been perfect and he showed it throughout the fight. Hugh O'Neil was thirty-two years of age and had the advantage of fifty-two pounds weight and two inches in height, being altogether the larger and more powerful man; thick set, cool, of unflinching nerve, and great bodily strength. The betting was altogether in his favor as it seemed impossible to hope that a man of Orem's size could contest the fight with him successfully. Hugh was not so firm of flesh as Orem, and had dissipated to some extent while Orem had never taken a drink of intoxicating liquor or used tobacco.

At twenty minutes to two o'clock, time was called and quickly each man toed the mark and the battle begun and lasted three hours and five minutes, in which one hundred eighty-five rounds were fought. At this junction a sudden feeling seemed to animate the backers of both men. The referee was called on by both parties to stop the fight. (The men themselves were still game and ready to go.) This was accordingly done to the satisfaction of most people present. Bets were declared off and the ring money was divided evenly.

During the winter of 1864 a company of St. Paul men organized the Idaho Steam Packet Company and purchased two steamers, the "Chippeway Falls" and the "Cutter." Their object was to establish a route from Minnesota to the gold mines at the headwaters of the Missouri (as all the great northwestern country was then called). The company advertised to take passengers to the newly discovered mines in ninety days. Both boats were outfitted and started from La Crosse on April 18, 1865, with two hundred and fifty passengers on board and quite an amount of freight. The boats proceeded without trouble, making excellent time, until they reached Fort Randal.

The government had sent General Sully against the Sioux and he was seriously handicapped for lack of means of transportation and on May 10 impressed the "Chippeway Falls" to carry supplies for his expedition. All the passengers and freight were transferred to the "Cutter" and, although overloaded and most uncomfortably crowded, she made her way to Fort Benton and discharged her passengers and freight. Here she was deserted by crew and engineers, who ran off to the mines, and the boat was tied up for the rest of the summer.

The "Chippeway Falls" was ordered down the river to "light off" a steamer loaded with expeditionary stores, which was on its way up to General Sully, and join him at Fort Randal. Sully moved on the east side of the Missouri, the "Chippeway Falls" following near him along the river until the expedition reached a point near the Cannon Ball river.   Here the "Chippe-way" ferried the troops across and then started for a point, designated by General Sully, on the Yellowstone river, where was one of Manuel Lisa's old trading posts.

The "Chippeway Falls" was to carry provisions and forage to this point in company with a steamer called the "Alone."   General Sully started back with an Indian guide and as they could not carry with them many rations or much forage it was of utmost importance that the boat reach the point named on time.

Captain Hutchinson with sixty-five thousand rations and accompanied by the "Alone," started on up the Missouri and soon reached Fort Union at the mouth of the Yellowstone.   Here he left the "Alone" and his cargo and started up the Yellowstone on an exploring expedition.

Captain Hutchinson ran up only about fifty miles on this trip, but finding about four feet of water pronounced navigation on the Yellowstone practicable and returned for his consort and freight.   Leading again, the "Chippeway Falls" attended by the "Alone" started up the Yellowstone.   This time they ascended to the old trading post at the mouth of the Big Horn,[100] where they waited for the troops six days.   The "Alone" grounded six miles below the post and could go no further.

Sully's troops had been on half rations for several days and were rejoiced to see the boats.   The animals were also starving; many had been abandoned and killed.   After having recruited their strength, Captain

---

[100] This post was first established by Manuel Lisa about 1807 and was known as Fort Lisa. Later it was renamed Fort Benton. Chittenden, *American Fur Trade*, vol. i, p. 150 n. After 1850 it was known as the Big Horn post. – ED.

Hutchinson ferried them across the Yellowstone and descended to Fort Union.

The expedition finally went down the river to Fort Berthold,[101] here Captain Hutchinson was released from government service and took the "Chippeway Falls" to St. Joseph, Missouri. So it was that, the "Chippeway Falls," which drew about thirteen inches of water when light, commanded by Capt. Abraham Hutchinson, was the first steamer whose paddles ever stirred the waters of the Yellowstone.

Early in the spring of 1865 an attempt was made to build a town on the Missouri at the mouth of the Marias, where steamboats could land and discharge their freight and thus save twenty miles of shallow and difficult navigation between there and Fort Benton. The Ophir Townsite Company surveyed a town and offered lots for sale. A steam sawmill was purchased and men sent down to get out logs, preparatory to building a town. On May 25, while at work in the timber three miles from the landing, ten men were surprised by a band of one hundred Blackfoot Indians and all were massacred. Four of the men were scalped. The Indians made a hasty retreat and crossed the line into British territory before they could be overtaken and punished.

In 1865 the sole medium of exchange in Montana was gold dust. The few greenbacks and treasury notes brought into the country by emigrants were a commodity, and bought and sold at market price. Mer-

---

[101] Old Fort Berthold was built by the American Fur Company about 1845. In 1862 it was moved to a nearby location on the Missouri river near the present Fort Berthold Indian reservation. In 1864 government troops were stationed there and it was important in the Sioux war. It was abandoned in 1867. *South Dakota Historical Collections*, vol. i (1902) p. 134.— ED.

chants usually made one trip east during the year; taking with them the year's accumulation of gold dust with which to pay their obligations and to purchase additional goods.

During the winter of 1865 a number of trains from Salt Lake, loaded with flour were snowed in in Beaver cañon and all the oxen perished in the storm. Provisions of every kind became scarce. Potatoes sold for 65c per pound, bacon $1.00 per pound, sugar 85c, tea $3.00, butter $1.75, candles 90c per pound, beans 40c, soap 50c, hominy 75c and flour $27.00 per cwt. On the twentieth of February there was a big raise in the price of flour from $27.00 to $40.00 and up and up until it had reached $150.00 per cwt. Most people, especially those with families, were unable to purchase flour at that price and as all provisions were scarce, many were reduced to a diet of meat straight. Beef was quite plentiful and sold for fifteen cents per pound. It was evident that a corner was held on flour. Groups of people collected on the streets and the all absorbing topic of conversation was the price of flour.

On April 18 word came that a large body of men armed and well organized were marching up from Nevada with the avowed determination to take possession of all the flour in town and divide it among the citizens at a reasonable and fair price. This information was soon verified by the appearance of five hundred men marching in file, all armed with revolvers and rifles. This force was under a leader on horseback, carrying an empty sack nailed to a staff as a banner. The men were divided into six companies each commanded by a captain and moved in military fashion. There was no doubt of their intentions: within five minutes after their arrival they commenced at the foot of Wallace street and searched every store and place where flour could be concealed. About one hundred twenty-five sacks were found and safely stored away in Leviathan hall. The search was orderly but very thorough and disclosed sundry lots of flour concealed under coats, in boxes and barrels and under hay stacks. An armed force determined to have all the flour that could be found in stores or the property of dealers wherever hidden and yet going through the matter as quietly as if it were a seizure by order of the court.

The men took no notice of people on the streets or of remarks addressed to them but followed after their captain; halted, fronted, and stood like a provost guard while the leader made known his business and detailed a party for the search. This being completed, if flour was found it was packed off without ceremony; an account being kept and a promise to pay for all at the rate of $27.00 per cwt. for Salt Lake flour and $36.00 for states flour. A notice was handed in to the *Montana Post* ordering all flour to be sold from $27.00 to $30.00 for the future.

A meeting was held in Leviathan hall in the evening: representation having been made of three cases in one of which flour had been taken from a boarding-house keeper and another in which a baker's stock had been confiscated and in a third where flour had been taken from a family. The complaints were investigated and the flour returned next day. A number of dissatisfied citizens and flour dealers held a meeting in the court room in the evening, but no action was taken.

On Wednesday the distribution of the flour was begun: twelve pounds were issued to a man who was willing to affirm that he had no flour and was unable to procure any; a double ration was given to a married man, and more in case there were children. A barrier guarded by armed men was placed at the door of the flour depot. The men were admitted to the hall in squads of ten. At the instance of Mayor Pfouts the committee promised that any flour brought in by pack train from Snake river or Salt Lake City should be sold at a price not to exceed fifty dollars per cwt. unless proof of its costing more be made.

Some of the citizens became much annoyed by the vigor of the search but upon the whole there was but little ill-feeling. On Thursday the committee paid for all the flour that they had taken, at the rate of $27.00 per cwt. George Mann, J. T. Sullivan, Joseph Marion, John Creighton, Ming and North, and Kercheval and Company were the principal holders of flour. After the flour was distributed the members of the committee returned to their homes.

During the winter (1866-67) Governor Smith inaugurated the custom of holding weekly levees in the council chamber, at Virginia City. Governor Smith assisted by Mr. Thomas Frances Meagher received the guests. These were the first exclusive gatherings in the territory. Guests were admitted by invitation cards only.

On September 22, 1866, occurred the death of our beloved friend Professor Dimsdale. This gentle, kind-hearted, Christian man came among us in the summer of 1863. A man of culture and refinement he drew to himself all that was best of society at that time in Virginia City. He organized and taught the first school in the territory, was the first superintendent of public instruction and edited the first newspaper published in the territory. He published *The Vigilantes* an absolutely correct narrative of the operations of that society.

Of an extremely delicate constitution the arduous duties and close confinement attendant on managing and editing a newspaper undermined his health, and he died at the early age of thirty-five, mourned by all who knew him.

While in Benton on August 29, 1866, a freight wagon drawn by four mules and escorted by a company of miners, arrived. The wagon was loaded with two and one-half tons of gold dust, valued at one million five hundred thousand dollars. The gold was all from Confederate gulch and was shipped down the river by steamboat. This was the first and only time that I ever saw a wagon load of gold dust at one time.

This same year a tanning mill was located on Mill creek about twenty-five miles from Virginia City. The bark was ground by water power and they were able to tan about two thousand cow hides during the summer. This mill was in successful operation for about five years and turned out an excellent quality of leather.

In 1866 a telegraph line was completed from Salt Lake City to Virginia City, Montana.

In the fall of 1867 I sold the business in Virginia City to F. E. W. Patten and took up my permanent residence in Deer Lodge.

Quartz Mining and Railroads

The next few years were busy ones for me. We were engaged in mining at Argenta and Philipsburg, had a store and lumber yard at Deer Lodge and a store in Philipsburg. The quartz mill at Philipsburg was completed and put in operation on October 2, 1867. We had spent large sums of money and two years of time on this enterprise and had employed meteorologists and chemists of national reputation, but when the mill was put in operation it would not save the values in the ores. My brother James again spent the winter in St. Louis purchasing additional machinery, and the following summer made another trial but without success and we were obliged to abandon the enterprise.

In the spring of 1870 James was appointed post trader at Fort Browning [102] and went over into eastern Montana and I was left alone to look after the business in Deer Lodge which consisted of various mining enterprises, a ranch with a limited number of horses and cattle, a lumber yard and a mercantile establishment.

In addition to our private business I was county commissioner and school trustee and devoted no little time to county and school affairs.

From 1865 to 1870 was an era of great prosperity in Deer Lodge county. During this period the placer

---

[102] Fort Browning was a government fort in northeastern Montana, the agency post for the Assiniboine and Upper Sioux. Abandoned in 1873 when the Assiniboine agency was moved to Fort Belknap sixty miles above on the Milk river and the Sioux agency was moved to Fort Peck. – ED.

mines produced more than $20,000,000 in gold dust from gulches as follows:

Gold creek	$2000000
Ophir	5000000
McClellan	1600000
Lincoln	1200000
French gulch	1000000
German gulch	3000000
Nevada	
Jefferson	
Washington	1500000
Bear gulch	2600000
Scattering	2000000

The valleys were well settled with prosperous ranchers. The town of Deer Lodge was the center of education and refinement for the territory. Many families moved to town and built beautiful homes because of the superior educational advantages offered for their children. Every branch of business was represented by large and substantial establishments.

In August, 1870, L. E. Graham and J. B. Taylor arrived in Deer Lodge valley with four hundred and fifty heifers and five bulls of pure Durham blood. The cattle were purchased at Omaha, Nebraska, shipped to Ogden, Utah, and from there driven north. This was the first herd of thoroughbred cattle brought to Montana. During the summer of 1870 many wagons loaded with melons, tomatoes, cucumbers, green corn, and apples were hauled from the Bitter Root valley and sold in Deer Lodge.

In May, 1869, Miss Guine Evans, daughter of Morgan Evans, filed on one hundred and sixty acres of land on Warm Spring creek. This was the first homestead entry made by a woman in Montana. Miss Evans lived on her homestead and proved up on it and was granted a government patent to the land.

Virginia City was not what could be called a quiet town at this particular time. In addition to the members of the legislature there were numerous lobbies from various sections of the territory, the strongest one being the one in the interest of the railroad subsidy bill. These gentlemen were liberal entertainers and liquid refreshments flowed across the hotel bars as freely as the waters over Alder gulch. These revels were kept up all night long and after the legislature was in session it was no uncommon thing for the sergeant at arms to be sent through the legislative halls to arouse the drowsy members when a vote was being taken on some important bill.

Governor Potts and secretary, James E. Calloway were appointed by President Grant and were both Republicans while the legislature was solidly Democratic but the session passed without the friction between the executive and legislative branches that had marred previous sessions.

The question of the permanent location of the capitol arose. Deer Lodge was a strong candidate for that honor. There was much bitter feeling between the contending towns. Cartooning came into vogue for the first time in Montana. James M. Cavanaugh, our one time delegate in Congress, in a speech sarcastically referred to our splendid city of Deer Lodge as "the little village on the trail to Bear" and to this day (1915) the appellation has stuck.

From 1866 up to 1872 every legislature had passed laws voting extra compensation to United States and territorial officers out of the territorial treasury.

$282976.00 had been so expended and the financial condition of the territory had been badly involved, the indebtedness being over $500000.

The railroad subsidy bill was not favored by the governor and it did not pass although its friends kept up a bitter fight throughout the entire session. No sooner had the legislature adjourned than the railroad subsidy ring begun clamoring for an extra session, the nominal excuse being the imperfection of laws passed by the regular session. The real reason was the determination of the railroad subsidy crowd to pledge the territory to an exceedingly heavy subsidy to build a north and south railroad. Deer Lodge county strongly opposed the calling of an extra session. In March, 1873, Governor Potts did call an extra session to convene on April 14, 1873.

From 1870 to 1880 was a period of financial depression in Montana. Until 1870 placer mining was the all important industry in the territory: but from that time gold production decreased rapidly from all the old placers and there were no important new discoveries. Many of our leading citizens thought it time to abandon the country to the Indians and buffalo and not a few did leave for the states and for the new gold discoveries of the Black hills.

The Cheyenne, Arapaho, and Sioux Indians driven north and west from Kansas and Minnesota united under the able leadership of the great chief Red Cloud, harrassed the Missouri river transportation and emigrant trains to Montana and raided our ranches at will. For a time it did look as though the Indians would take possession whether we were willing or not.

Important discoveries of quartz ledges of gold, silver, and copper had been made and we had vast coal beds. Carefully kept weather records and considerable experimentation had proven that agriculture could be carried on successfully in all of our valleys but none of these resources could be developed without cheaper and better transportation facilities; a railroad into the territory became a necessity. How to get one at a cost that would not bankrupt the new and sparsely settled territory engaged the minds of the thoughtful citizens.

There were three possible chances to be considered. A north and south line to connect with the Union Pacific, an extension of the Utah Northern narrow gauge north from Snake river, Idaho, or the Northern Pacific transcontinental line across the territory east and west. This latter route was most feasible and to it we pinned our faith until the panic of 1873 carrying Jay Cooke and Company to the wall shattered our hopes in that direction.

All of the railroad subsidy bills introduced in the earlier legislatures called for sums of money sufficient to construct the proposed roads without other assistance and were entirely beyond what the territory should be expected to pay. Governor Potts who was an able lawyer held that the legislature had no legal power to bond the territory to subsidize a railroad and for that reason strongly opposed any act in that direction.

Meetings were held in different counties and committees appointed to solicit propositions from the Utah Northern and the Union Pacific looking to their early entrance into Montana.

John Young, a son of Brigham Young of Utah, was constructing a narrow gauge road northward into Idaho and offered to extend the line, three hundred miles to the mouth of the Big Hole river in Montana, the same to be completed in three years, for a consideration of

$5000 per mile. When the ninth session of the territorial legislature convened on January 3, 1876, a law was passed authorizing an election whereby qualified voters could pass on issuing $1500000, of territorial bonds to contribute toward the construction of a railroad from Franklyn, Idaho, to Big Hole river in Montana.

Another act authorizing counties to be benefited thereby, to submit to the voters the proposition of issuing bonds to aid a railroad and still another act allowing counties through which the Northern Pacific railroad would pass to call elections whereby voters could decide on bonding the said counties to aid that road was passed.

At the election, bonds for a railway subsidy failed to carry and in April, 1877, Sidney Dillon, president of the Utah Northern made a proposition to the Governor of Montana, to extend the line into Montana and Governor Potts called an extra session of the legislature to consider the proposition. Before a special election to vote on bonds could be held the road crossed the Montana border and was being pushed northward as rapidly as possible. The Utah Northern narrow gauge was completed to Silver Bow in 1880 and a branch extended to Garrison in 1881.

Life and Customs of the Indians

The first years of my residence in Montana were spent west of the Rocky mountains and the Indians I came in contact with were the Shoshones, Bannocks, Flatheads, Kalispells, Kootenais, Spokanes, and Nez Percés. Their life and habits became to me an interesting study and as all of these tribes were friendly and constantly camped near us I had a good opportunity to study them.

Each tribe had a head chief and several sub chiefs. The head chieftainship was sometimes hereditary, but more often he was elected by the council. His authority was almost despotic, although when questions of unusual importance arose the head chief called a council of all the sub chiefs, and head men of the tribe. Much attention is given to the advice of old men of the tribe.

The war chiefs were elected because of some unusual feat of bravery or daring. Any young man of a tribe could become war chief if he possessed the requisite qualifications. The war chief was often selected for a season but held his place so long as he excelled all others of the tribe in waging successful war against their enemies and in bringing home the greatest number of stolen ponies.

After each successful battle there would be a war dance. A fire would be built in the open and all the warriors present assembled. The scalps taken were placed on a long pole and stuck up near the fire. The women and young boys formed an outer circle and were spectators but never took any part in the dance. The war chief opened the dance by standing up and reciting the deeds of bravery, then all the warriors would form in a sort of promenade around the fire chanting their war songs. Then another brave would recount his exploits and so on until each one had been heard or until they were all exhausted. On occasions when there had been a big fight and many scalps taken and few lives lost on their side, the war dance would be kept up for three or four nights.

Indians believed implicitly in magic. Each tribe had its medicine man. He occupied a tent by himself and spent much time in solitude, conjuring up magical powers to bring success to the tribe, to keep away evil spirits, to prevent misfortune and to heal the sick. He usually had a highly ornamental parflash, in which he kept one or more fetishes. Sometimes it was a small bush or herb and again it was a queer-shaped stone, a piece of hair or a bear's claw. No one excepting the medicine man dared to go near or touch the sacred parflash.

The medicine man was always consulted before the tribe engaged in an enterprise of any magnitude. If he was successful the medicine was considered strong and the medicine man rose in tribal favor, but if unsuccessful the medicine was considered weak and the dispenser thereof must get to work and improve his brand or he would soon be discarded altogether. Most of the medicine men were sagacious old fellows and managed to keep their positions unless the tribe had a very hard run of luck. Some of them like old Winnemucca and Sitting Bull gained an influence that transcended that of head chief.

These tribes also had sort of shrines usually a tree or some peculiarly shaped rock on which they placed gifts to the Great Spirit. There was one large pine tree on top of the hill just west of McCary's bridge in Hell Gate cañon, on which the Indians hung small articles of bead work, bear claws, strips of red cloth, queer-shaped stones, bunches of white sage, pieces of buffalo scalp, small pieces of bone, etc. There was another such tree in the Bitter Root valley fifty miles above Stevensville. The objects were hung on these trees as the Indians passed on their way out to the hunting grounds and were placed there to invoke the aid of the Great Spirit to make game plentiful and to make them successful in their enterprises.

In the big bend of Milk river thirty miles east of Fort Belknap is a big gray granite rock resembling a buffalo lying down. This rock was greatly reverenced by the Blackfeet and River Crows and in passing they always placed on it some talisman. Many of them made long pilgrimages to this sacred rock for the sole purpose of making offerings.

Another sacred rock was a huge red sandstone boulder on the side of a grassy bluff on the northwest of Fort Benton. This huge rock once rested on the top of the bluff but as the rains and snows washed the soft gravely earth from around it, it gradually slipped down the hillside. Indians are very observing and as they noticed the changed position of the huge rock on the hillside they attributed it to something supernatural and it became a sacred shrine to them. In addition to placing objects on these rocks, they often carved or painted figures or characters on the rocks.

The sun dance was the great annual reunion of the tribe and was the most important ceremony of the plains' Indians. It was held late in the summer or autumn, first before the big or fall buffalo hunt. The head chief decided the time and place for this meeting and every member of the tribe was present.

The great village was arranged in a semi-circle with the opening toward east. The head chief directed the placing of the tepees but they were arranged with reference to the rank and influence of the families in the tribe. At one side and some little distance from the outskirts of the village were placed three or four tepees for the exclusive use of the medicine men. These tepees were sacred and no one but the occupants must go near them.

As soon as the tribe had gathered the medicine men retired to these tepees and remained there fasting and in meditation and in preparing talismans and in the performance of secret rites. This finished, preparations for the erection of the big lodge are begun. This lodge is always placed in the center of the semi-circle but the exact spots where the center pole and altar is to be placed is selected and consecrated by the big medicine man of the tribe, with much ceremony.

The center pole is selected and prepared by young men, members of a secret society and no one else must touch the sacred pole. Around this center pole is placed a roofless lodge one hundred feet in diameter and about eight feet high with the opening toward the east. As soon as the big lodge is up the medicine men and those who are to dance go inside and spend the night fasting, meditating, and in dedicating the lodge.

On the following morning the altar is prepared at the west side of the lodge. An oval-shaped hole is scraped out about six inches deep and in this is placed

braided wisps of sweetgrass, sage, willows, or juniper
and around it about four inches apart is set a row of
brilliantly-colored willow sticks; behind this is placed
an elaborate arrangement of buffalo skulls, elk and
deer horns.

This finished the medicine men begin to paint and
adorn the naked bodies of the dancers by smearing
them with grease paint and placing wisps of willow
and sage about their heads, necks, arms, waists, and
ankles.

Those who are candidates for warriors have slits cut
in their flesh underneath the shoulder blades and
through this is passed a rawhide rope or thong to the
ends of which is attached three or four buffalo skulls
that drag on the ground behind the dancer until the
flesh gives way and he is released.

At the south end of the lodge six or seven musicians
sit around a large drum and when all is ready the
musicians begin beating the drum and chanting, the
dancers form a circle and the dancing begins, all blowing on a whistle made from the quill of an eagle's wing.
The dancing and the noise is kept up for hours or until
all the buffalo skulls have torn loose from the flesh.   It
is considered a piece of great cowardice to be released
in any other way, and the one who can endure the greatest torture for the longest period of time ranks highest
as a warrior.

These dances are not only for tests of valor but they
are for the purpose of calling up Chinook winds, driving away evil spirits, making game plentiful, averting
lightning and pestilences, and to give luck to the warriors, gamblers, and horse thieves.   At the conclusion
of this dance the participants take an emetic and then
go to the sweat house.

After this comes the feast of commemoration for the dead. The men who have lost relatives or friends during the year, dance and chant death songs. If a head chief has died or been killed the whole tribe joins in the ceremony. His son recites his deeds of valor before the dancing begins. When this is finished the big council starts. The head chief presides. The rank of chiefs and warriors is decided, tribal differences settled, and new policies inaugurated.

At the close of the big council there are banquets among the chief's relatives and friends and the social dance in which both men and women take part and there is always a number of weddings.

The duration of the social festivities is determined largely by the condition of the commissary. If pemmican, fat dogs, smoked buffalo tongue, and like delicacies were plentiful they lasted a week or until they were all eaten up, then the families all pack up and leave to follow their every day pursuits.

The center pole and the altar are always left standing. They are considered sacred and must not be disturbed.

The tepee always belongs to the Indian man, but it is the woman who provides it and forever looks after it. Constructing an Indian lodge was no small undertaking.

First of all there is the skin covering to prepare. In 1858 the most used covering was made from the elk skin. The squaw skinned the animal, then folding it carefully, carried it, with the meat to the camp. The man's work began and ended with the killing of the animal. If horses were plentiful the woman was allowed a pack horse to bring in the meat and hide, but if scarce she carried it in on her back. The skin was then stretched out and pinned securely to the ground with wooden pegs and then with a piece of elk horn sharpened much like a chisel she would go over every particle of the hide scraping and removing any particle of flesh that adhered to it.   Then turning it over and hanging it over a pole which was placed slanting against a tree, she took a buffalo rib and scraped all the hair and scriffin from the other side.   This was a long tedious operation as they had only a little strip about three inches wide and a foot long to work on when the skin would have to be shifted.   It would often require weeks to get the hair off of one hide.   After both sides of a skin was thus prepared, the next thing was to go all over it with a cobble rock split in two; with the sharp edge of this rock they rubbed and pounded and worked the skin until it was soft.   It was again stretched on the ground, the brains were melted and poured over it and thoroughly rubbed in.   It was then left in the sun until the brain substance was absorbed. It was again taken up and washed in warm water until it was thoroughly clean and white, then wrung out and rubbed and stretched and pounded until it was perfectly dry.   Four skins were then fastened together like a square box.   A hole was dug in the ground and filled with pieces of bark or dead wood and set on fire.   This would make little heat, but a dense smoke.   Over the hole they would place a tripod and inside of that were hung the skins spread out well over the hole so that the smoke would reach every part of them.   When skins were well smoked they were a beautiful light brown, soft as cloth and would never after become hard when wet.   Elk, deer, antelope, and mountain sheep skins were dressed in this way.

It required from ten to twelve elk skins to make a

lodge and these had to be cut and sewed together with sinew; all the little holes for the sinew were punched with an awl.

Next was the preparing of the frame work. This required from twelve to fourteen poles, twelve or sixteen feet long and three inches in diameter at the bottom, tapering somewhat toward the top. It is some trouble to get exactly the right kind of lodge poles so the camp usually make a trip to some well-known spot where the right kind of poles could be found. Here they camp and allow the squaws to get and prepare a quantity sufficient to do all hands for some time. The poles are carefully peeled and laid out straight to dry. Then a hole is burned in each one about twenty inches from the top. This is to enable them to tie them together in bunches of six or seven so they can be fastened, one bunch on either side of the saddle with the other end dragging along the ground. In this way they are moved when the camp is traveling.

The men ride ahead and select camping places. When there is a large village the chief directs the placing of the tepees. The women then erect three poles which are fastened together with leather thongs. The top of the skin covering is fastened to the tops of these poles and then raised and stood up like a tripod, the other poles are next placed in the crotches of these three poles and when all are placed and the elk skin covering drawn around them a squaw enters the lodge and pushes the bottom of the poles out in a circle until the skin is stretched perfectly tight over the poles; they then fasten it securely around the bottom with wooden pegs. These pegs are carried with them and there is always a supply on hand. The only openings to the lodge are at the top where the poles project, and a small opening about three feet square cut in one side of the lodge about one foot from the ground, used for an entrance and over this opening is hung a deer skin stretched on a wood frame. This is kept shut in cold weather, but is always open when warm.

The fire is built in the center of the lodge and the smoke escapes through the small opening at the top. Two poles six inches in diameter are placed three feet apart from the door to the fire. This is the entrance.

To the right of the door and occupying one-fourth of the lodge is the woman's department; here are the small children and whatever cooking utensils and sewing materials the lodge affords. No visitor ever trespasses in this part of the lodge. The floor of the rest of the space is covered with rye grass or willow twigs. All around the circle is placed the tanned robes, and parflashes containing the dried meats, pemmican, dried roots, and berries, dressed skins and in fact everything belonging to the family. The family spread their robes on the rye grass and sleep in a circle with their feet to the fire.

A lodge the size of the one described will accommodate a family of ten. Girls remain in their parents' lodge until married, sleeping on the same side of the circle with the mother, but the boys leave the home lodge early and live apart five or six in one lodge. Brothers often remain together, but sometimes a lodge is made up of cousins or friends. The mother and sisters provide the lodges, move, and set up these bachelor apartments.

Some of the lodges were painted and decorated with colored drawings; these drawings represented victorious battles or horse-stealing raids and some of them were very cleverly executed. The coloring was always harmonious and pleasing. When an Indian possessed one of these decorated lodges he would not sell it. I doubt if there is one of them in existence today.

A good elk skin lodge is a very comfortable thing to live in. The opening in the top, while very small, would let in no rain or snow, and was a perfect ventilator, letting out all smoke and bad air. A very little fire kept it warm and in summer time it is raised up about two feet all around the bottom. This allows the air to pass and keeps it perfectly cool. All the cooking is done outside, unless the weather is very bad. I do not remember of ever having a cold while living in an elk skin lodge.

The women do all of the work even to saddling and unsaddling the horses for their lords and masters. Girls are taught to do all the work which falls to the mother's lot, when they are very young. When game was plentiful hundreds of animals, deer, sheep, elk, and buffalo, were killed and the women dressed all the skins and dried all the meat beside the regular routine work of camp life.

The moving of an Indian village is an interesting sight. The herders bring in all the ponies; each one selects his own and the saddling up begins. Some of the men saddle their own ponies, but more often the women do it for them. Next the lodges are dismantled, parflashes, and robes, and extra baggage are packed on pack horses. The lodge poles are tied in bundles of from four to six each, and a bunch tied on either side of the saddle, the other end dragging on the ground. On these poles and about two feet from the ground is piled the lodge covering, cooking utensils and robes or skins or dried meat. These things are all lashed on securely and ride along as easily as though they were in a wagon. This is called a travois. In this way one pony will drag one hundred fifty to two hundred pounds.

The parflash is a box made of rawhide in which is carried dried roots, sugar or salt, if the village had any, and any small articles like red paint, beads, elk teeth, porcupine quills, or things likely to get lost or be injured by getting wet. These parflashes are usually packed on pack horses, and often small children are packed on with them. Boys and girls old enough to ride have their own ponies, two or three children ride on one pony. The infants are strapped to a papoose board and this board hung over the pommel of the mother's saddle, from where the little thing dangles during the long marches.

When all is ready the cavalcade advances, first the chiefs and braves, then the younger members of the village, then pack horses and travois, children, and last the squaws and dogs. Not that the dogs rank with the squaws! A dog is a valuable asset in an Indian village, he is night watch and then his flesh is considered a dish of great delicacy. He travels with the squaws from choice, he knows that the nearer he is to the squaws, the nearer to the commissary.

When I first came among these Indians they had plenty of good horses, clean new blankets, much red cloth, and gay-hued calicoes. The chiefs sported the most gorgeous war bonnets, highly embroidered and beaded buckskin suits, and moccasins. A moving village was a most entertaining and picturesque sight.

When streams were high they constructed boats by making a round basket shaped frame work of willows and then stretching buffalo hides tightly over that they had a fairly good boat in which two could paddle themselves across nicely. They also spread out the lodge skins and packing everything inside drew the skin up tight and tied it. This made a large balloon shaped bundle and with a rawhide rope attached to the top, was then placed in the stream and a woman and two or three small children would be perched on top clinging to the rope. An Indian with a pony, that was a good swimmer, would take hold of the end of the rope and start out across the stream. The queer-looking bundle would bob and bounce around in the swift current, but the pony would finally make the shore and land everybody safely and comparatively dry. Whole villages would cross the largest, swiftest, streams during flood waters and I do not remember of ever hearing of one drowning, although many white men lost their lives in attempting to cross the same streams.

An Indian could have as many wives as he wished and many of them had three, but seldom did they have more than five. Usually the chief took the captives, but if the captive was a woman she was turned over to the women of the tribe to be tortured to death or made a slave and compelled to do the drudgery of the camp.

Wherever there is an Indian village there is a number of sweat houses. These are constructed out of willow bushes made round about seven feet in diameter and four feet high. Over this they spread robes or blankets and inside build a fire and heat a pile of cobble rocks. When the rocks are red hot they scratch out the fire and provide themselves with a bucket of cold water, strip and crawl into this small wickiup and pour the cold water over the hot rocks. This creates a dense steam and makes it suffocatingly hot. The occupant remains here as long as he can stand it, then he comes out takes a run to the nearest stream and plunges into icy water. The sweat house is the Indian remedy for all illnesses. When smallpox first appeared among them, many lost their lives by using this treatment.

The Catholic missionaries had come among these Indians before I arrived and most of them had embraced that faith. This was especially true of the Flatheads but before that they were sun worshippers. When an Indian tried to convince you, he invariably pointed to the sun and said "The Great Spirit, the sun knows I do not lie." Through all their legends the sun is the Great Spirit and is given power over all other spirits.

The tribes of western Montana were hospitable, truthful, and scrupulously honest, until the whites taught them otherwise. Horse stealing was a legitimate game among all the tribes and a clever horse thief ranked with a sub chief.

The women of some tribes were virtuous, in others the men traded wives as readily as they traded horses and virtue was unknown. The Nez Percé were the highest type of Indian that I met with and the Crows the lowest. I have found little in the Crows to commend.

Among all the tribes the women were sold. The young people more or less made their choice, but when a man takes an Indian girl he is expected to leave a good horse, some blankets, and trinkets at her father's lodge when he takes her away. If she is a particularly attractive girl he will leave two or more horses.

I have had letters from eastern people asking me if I could furnish them copies of Indian love songs – I have read of Indian love songs but never heard any such songs among the Montana tribes. The only songs I ever heard them sing were their war songs, and a peculiar chant which they kept up while gambling, for the purpose of making them lucky at the game. Should the strains of a war song reach the ear of an Indian maiden she generally climbed a tree or crawled into a convenient hole until the warbler drifted out of her neighborhood. A war song is one of the most ear-splitting, blood-curdling howls that ever reached my ear and they are only indulged in when a battle is being waged.

If a "brave" wishes to attract the attention of some particular Indian maiden he usually dresses up and does some fancy riding stunts, on his best pony, in the vicinity of her father's tepee, or kills an unusual lot of game, or drives his share of stolen ponies past her door, or displays some fresh scalps on his con stick. I have seen young couples sauntering around on the outskirts of a village looking as silly as white couples do, but not often.

At a very early age the Indian boy is taught the art of war, the chase, and horse stealing. He can use a bow and arrow almost as soon as he can walk. He practices all sorts of fights to cultivate bravery and cunning. His standing in the tribe depends upon his acts of bravery and his cunning at capturing horses belonging to an enemy. The young men usually follow the advice of old men of the tribe but it is not difficult for him to become a sub chief if he is a clever hunter, skilled horseman, and brave in the face of danger.

The little girls play with dolls and make pets of the puppies, often binding the little fellows on a papoose board and carrying them on their back in imitation of their mothers carrying the baby. At a very early age the girls are instructed in all the arts of their home life, sewing, bead work, dressing skins, etc.

A young girl's entrance into womanhood was attended with much ceremony. A place was selected in a dense thicket or grove near a stream, and some distance from the village. Here a small tepee would be erected. The mother of the maiden would then instruct her in a code of ethics, which would affect her whole after-life. She must sit erect in the center of the tepee lest she become lazy, she must fast lest she become gluttonous. She must not speak lest she become garrulous. Her meditations must be on obedience to her parents, speaking the truth, kindness and gentleness and being a dutiful wife and a good mother.

With these instructions she retires to the tepee and there remains in solitude for four or five days. During this time she does much bathing and before leaving the tepee she is given wisps of sweetgrass, white sage or pine needles with which she builds a smudge, then leaning over it allows the smoke to envelop her then standing erect in the smoke she faces the sun and extending her arms above her head chants a sort of prayer. Her mother then brings her new clothing and when dressed she would leave the tepee and return to her home.

In every Indian village there is one very old man who will tell stories to the children and at this tepee the children love to gather and they are as anxious for the legends as are the white children for the fairy tales told them when gathered about the open grate at home.

There is one legend told, with some few variations, by almost every tribe of Indians in Montana. It was given to me by a Nez Percé boy and here it is just as he told it to me.

It appears there was at one time a great giant who lived in the valley of Kamiah (Kam-yaph) Idaho.

This valley has been settled by the Nez Percé tribe of Indians so far back no one knows. The giant's head extended as far up as where the town of Kooskia now stands (or Indian name Tu-ku-pa). This clear water valley in the vicinity of Kamiah (Kam-yaph) Kooskia (or Tu-ku-pa) is the Garden of Eden of north Idaho. This giant was eight miles long and use to swallow every living thing that came in his way, and the coyote heard about it and he planned a scheme to kill this great giant. The coyote was just in the prime of life and was very popular and a great man among all the living beings at that time. It appears all the living creatures or animals at that time were supposed to be human beings and this coyote prophecied that the time was coming and this time was very short when new and more superior human beings would take their place, meaning the present human race. As stated above, coyote determined to kill the great giant, so he went to work and made him a rope from hemp, willow bark, etc., to tie himself and fasten these ropes to high mountains, such as Pilot Knob, Seven Devils, and other high mountains, and then he [coyote] stationed himself on top of the Whitebird hill, between Camas prairie and the Whitebird cañon, made a crown out of bunch grass so the giant could not see him or detect him. Then the coyote challenged the great giant to swallow him, but the giant could not see him. This giant had heard about the coyote being a very popular and a very hard man to be beaten.

The great giant challenged the coyote to swallow him [giant] first, but coyote insisted that the giant swallow him, so finally the great giant drew his breath and the coyote came jumping into the mouth of the great giant. Before the coyote allowed himself to be swallowed he secured a bunch of fir pitch and also secreted five flint spears or knives in his person. After coyote being swallowed first thing he came to was a rattlesnake and the snake wanted to bite him, made all kinds of hissing noise. Coyote stamped on the snake's head and flattened it, coyote said to snake if you were so brave and so dangerous why did you allow yourself to be swallowed by this giant and not do anything to save yourself and all that have been swallowed by this monster and allow him to rule over you. Coyote went further and the grizzly bear met him and growled at him and showed fight. Coyote treated him [grizzly] the same way as he did with the snake, kicked the grizzly in the nose, that turned grizzly's nose up, etc.

Coyote finally arrived at the giant's heart, first thing coyote did was to see that all living things got out of the giant and he kicked all the bones out, then he went to cutting the giant's heart, and built a fire with the fir pitch he brought with him. The giant began to feel the pain and begged coyote to let him alone and that he [giant] would allow him to go free, but coyote said, "No you swallowed men, and now you got to take the consequences." Coyote broke all his flint knives, but one with which he finished cutting in the heart. Before the giant died, coyote managed to get out. After the giant died, coyote took his last flint knife and cut the giant up and distributed different parts of the great giant's body all over North America and commanded that out of this giant's body shall be made different tribes of Indians.

When he had finished his partner, fox, said to him in his usual quiet way, "Coyote, you have forgotten this part of the country, and have not left any part of giant's flesh."

Coyote turned to fox and said, "You are always stupid, why did you not tell me before?" So coyote told fox to bring some water, for his hands were bloody. Coyote took the water and dipped his bloody hands and sprinkled the bloody water on the ground and commanded that out of said bloody water the Nez Percé tribe of Indians should come forth. Though the Nez Percé tribe may be a small tribe, they will be the most intelligent, bravest, and greatest fighters of any tribe in North America.

The Nez Percé name for the giant the coyote killed is "Iltz-wa-we-tsih."

About the only difference in the story is in the location of the valley. With the Nez Percé it is the valley of the Kamiah; with the Crows it is the valley of the Big Horn; with the Flatheads, it is the Mission valley.

Niñumbee is another very singular fairy tale told among the Snakes and Bannocks. It runs about as follows: In the Salmon River mountains there lives in caves among the rocks, a race of fairies, about two feet high, who, with bow in hand and arrow-case slung on their backs, go out and hunt and kill sheep, deer, elk, and antelope which they carry home on their backs; they eat the flesh, and their wives dress the skins, from which they make themselves clothes while the men go entirely naked.

Now whenever the Indians are in their vicinity, and a woman goes out after wood or for any other purpose, and happens to lay her infant down and gets out of sight of it, one of these fairies immediately devours it and taking its place, begins to cry at a terrible rate; the woman hearing her child, as she supposes, crying, returns, and taking it up gives it to suck to pacify it,

when it instantly seizes her by the breast and com-
mences devouring it.

Now these fairies are a kind of human "monitor"
being perfectly proof against knives, axes, stones, clubs,
or firearms, so the poor woman cannot get rid of him,
and her screams being heard by her husband or friends,
they rush to the spot, when the little devil takes to flight,
leaving her in a dying condition. She always dies before morning. If they leave her to go after more help
the fairy instantly returns and finishes the job by eating
her up altogether.

When these fairies see little children playing together a little way out of camp, one of them will take
his tail in his hand and gives it a wind around his body
to conceal it, will approach the children and want to
play with them. Sometimes they discover the tail and
take to flight and "save their bacon" but at other times
they do not notice it and let him come among them,
when first thing they known he "gobbles up" some little
"image of his dad," clasps him astride of his tail and
runs off with him, and that is the last that is ever seen
or heard of that unfortunate child.

Their cannibalistic propensities, however, do not
appear to extend to Indian men, for whenever they hap-
pen to meet one near their dwelling, they invite him in
and give him something to eat and insist on his staying
all night, but he invariably refuses; saying that he has
killed some game and must go and take it home or the
wolves will eat it. The general opinion, however, is,
that he is afraid to stay, but he scorns the imputation.

The fairies often gather together of an evening on
high rocks and cliffs and sing most boisterously, and
are supposed to be having a good time generally. They
are seldom seen except in the evening.

There is also another kind of these fairies that live in streams, and are called "pah-o-nah" which means, "water infants." They devour women and children in the same manner as the land fairies, and are malignant "little cusses."

Indian Wars of the Northwest

The summer of 1864 was the beginning of our trouble with hostile Indians. With the exception of the Blackfeet, the native Indians of Montana were not hostile and this tribe had confined their depredations to horse stealing and murdering an occasional lone trapper or prospector.

The Crows, the most treacherous and insolent of all the native tribes, professed friendship for the whites but never lost an opportunity to steal horses or murder white men if they got a chance. They were friendly only because it enabled them to trade for guns and ammunition and furnished them a powerful ally against their hereditary enemy, the Sioux.

In 1863 the Sioux, driven from Minnesota and Dakota, took refuge west of the Missouri and along the Yellowstone. Just at this period when the United States was in the throes of a civil war the British subjects, if not the government, along our northern border gave much aid and comfort to hostile Indians on both sides of the line; trading them quantities of arms and ammunition and furnishing a safe refuge for the hostile bands that fled north across the line whenever pursued by the whites. Most of the arms and ammunition in the hands of the hostile Sioux came from the British and half-breed traders across the line.

The brutal and entirely unjustifiable massacre of a village of five hundred friendly Arapahoes in Colorado by Col. John M. Chivington [103] drove the entire tribe of Arapahoes and Cheyennes to the war path. The campaign against them in Nebraska and Colorado sent those tribes to the southern tributaries of the Yellowstone. As the Indians were driven north and west so were the buffalo and other large game and this section of country became a veritable Indian paradise.

Red Cloud, as brave a warrior and able a diplomat as ever guided the destinies of the redmen, made his headquarters on Powder river and lost no time in taking advantage of the situation, but set about forming a confederation of all the Indian tribes east of the Rocky mountains and north of the Arkansas river. At this time he was twenty-six years old, an eloquent and impassioned orator and a natural-born leader. He was fully six feet tall, muscular, and active as a panther and as fine a horseman as the world could produce. His emissaries were to be found wherever there were Indians. They were in the camps of the Chippeways, with the Crows and Blackfeet; south among the Cheyennes and Arapahoes; west with the Shoshones. There was no tribe of Indians too small or too weak or too insignificant to escape the attention of this wily chief, whose purpose was to form a confederation of all the tribes and sweep the white man from the face of the earth. His was to be a war of extermination. At one time he had twenty thousand warriors in his confederation and at least ten thousand under his personal command.

Up to this time Red Cloud had refused to sign any treaties but had kept up a relentless war, murdering settlers, burning ranches, stealing stock, and falling

---

[103] The Chivington massacre is described in detail in Paxson, *Last American Frontier*, pp. 259-261. – ED.

upon outlying posts. The Sioux were particularly aggressive along the route of the Bozeman-Bridger road to Montana. Scarcely an emigrant train passed without being attacked and most of them were compelled to fight all the way from Laramie, Wyoming, to Virginia City, Montana.

In the spring of 1864, the government planned a campaign on an extensive scale against them, the object being to pursue and conquer them and to forever put a stop to their depredations. Early in July the expedition consisting of the 5th and 6th regiments of Iowa cavalry, the 30th Wisconsin infantry, the 8th Minnesota infantry mounted, six companies of 2nd cavalry, two sections of artillery, and a company of white and Indian scouts with Gen. Alfred Sully, an old and experienced Indian fighter, in command, crossed the Missouri river at the point where Fort Rice now is and began the construction of that fort. Accompanying the command was a supply train of three hundred government teams and three hundred beef steers. Fifteen steamboats were loaded and started up the Missouri to distribute supplies and assist the troops along the course of the Missouri and Yellowstone rivers. An emigrant train of one hundred sixty teams and two hundred fifty people, men, women, and children bound for Montana, joined the expedition at Fort Rice.

At two o'clock on the afternoon of the twenty-eighth the scouts reported that they had located an extensive camp in the foot-hills of a low range of mountains along Knife river. They reported fifteen hundred lodges not three miles distant. The Indians discovered the advancing army about the same time that the scouts discovered them. Both sides began preparations for battle. General Sully dismounted the infantry and threw out a skirmish line with a reserve of cavalry to cover the flanks. The artillery was placed within supporting distance of the battle line.

The Indians showed no excitement but appeared to rather court a battle and seemed confident of being able to defeat the soldiers. They stripped for battle, mounted their war ponies and rode out to meet the foe. A few Indians rode up to almost within a gun shot, waving their war clubs and shouting defiance to the troops. At last the whole body mounted and came on a run directly at the battle line and discharging guns and arrows, wheeled and ran back to reload. The troops answered with a volley all along the line and the battle was on. The Indians repeated their charges again and again and fought with great bravery, but their guns were not as long ranged as the troops' and many of them were armed with nothing but bows and arrows. The battle lasted until sundown, when the artillery was brought into action and the troops moved forward, advancing toward the camp. So confident had the Indians been of success that not until this time had they made any attempt to save their camp. The first shell thrown into camp created the greatest confusion; women, children, and dogs swarmed from the tepees. The women rushed about midst bursting shells, tearing down lodges and removing contents. The voice of the war chief, rallying his braves sounded clear, above the cries of the women and children and the barking of the dogs. It was no use; the Indians were completely routed and their camp with most of their supplies was captured.

On the twenty-first of April, 1867, Thomas W. Cover returned to Bozeman bringing the intelligence of the murder of John M. Bozeman on April 16. Cover and

Bozeman had started for Forts C. F. Smith and Phil Kearney. They reached the Yellowstone without incident and had supper at Nelson Storey's cattle camp near Benson's landing. While there, five Indians drove off quite a bunch of horses, but Mitch Buoyer followed them and recovered all but one pony. Next morning Bozeman and Cover crossed the Yellowstone and followed down stream; camped for dinner on a little creek a few miles below the old Crow agency. While cooking their dinner they saw five Indians approaching camp on foot leading a pony. Both men picked up their rifles, Cover went over to the horses and Bozeman advanced toward the visitors. When they were within a hundred feet Bozeman said, "They are Crows, I know one of them." Cover was not so certain and began saddling his horse, Bozeman shook hands with the visitors and at that instant Cover saw one of the Indians move as though to bring his gun to play and called to Bozeman to shoot. The warning came too late. The Indians fired two balls striking Bozeman, one passing through him, and he fell dead. Cover fired and brought down one Indian but received a wound in the shoulder. He then took refuge in some choke-cherry bushes near camp, firing on the Indians as he retreated, but as his gun was not working well he missed his targets. Two of the Indians began saddling the horses while the other two kept firing at Cover concealed in the brush but they did not come close enough to hit him or to be in danger of his rifle. When the horses were ready the whole party mounted and rode away carrying their dead companion with them. Cover returned to camp to make certain that poor Bozeman was beyond all earthly help. The Indians did not scalp him or take his watch. Cover then made his way to Storey's camp where he was furnished a horse and taken to Bozeman. Nelson Storey and another man went to the scene of the disaster and buried Bozeman where he lay. These Indians were found later to be some renegade Blackfeet who had been expelled from their tribe and had taken refuge with the Crows.

The news of recent murders together with the report from a Bannock chief that the Bloods, Blackfeet, and Piegans had sent their squaws and children across the British line and were prepared to attack the Gallatin valley created the wildest excitement. Scouts were sent out to guard the passes and couriers to bring in all the women and children from the ranches. Everything pertaining to the militia was hurried forward. Several companies were enrolled at Bozeman at once and were ready to march under Colonel Thoroughman on receipt of orders. Virginia City sent out a company of cavalry and twenty-five special scouts. Helena boasted that Captain Lyons's company were in saddle and ready to march by May 14.

Early in May, 1867, Governor Meagher [104] appealed to the government for permission to muster in eight hundred citizens as a territorial battalion. General Sherman granted the request conditionally. Under it the work of preparation was carried forward rapidly and a military department organized.

About the middle of May, Mitch Buoyer and John Poiner, both half-breeds, arrived at Bozeman from Fort C. F. Smith and reported an alliance being

---

[104] General Meagher was appointed secretary of Montana Territory by President Johnson in 1865. He was never governor but in the frequent absence of the governor he was acting governor. Correspondence of Meagher in Bureau of Rolls and Library, Washington. Eulogy of Meagher by Martin Maginnis in *Montana Historical Society Contributions*, vol. vi. (Helena, 1907) pp. 102-118. Account of his death in *Ibid*, vol. viii (Helena, 1917) p. 131. – ED.

formed between the Sioux, Arapahoes, Cheyennes, and Gros Ventres; that they were holding sun dances on Powder river and would be on the war path about June first. They reported that the Indians claimed that there would be twenty thousand warriors in the field.

These men also brought word that there were but two hundred men at Fort Smith, that all of their horses had been killed or driven off by the Indians and that they were without provisions save a small quantity of corn which they boiled for food. The message stated that if they did not receive help immediately they would all perish.

Captain Hynson called for volunteers to go to the relief of Fort Smith and every man of his company stepped forward. An expedition was at once planned. Forty-two men, well-armed and equipped with ten wagons loaded with supplies, under command of Colonel De Lacey left Camp Elizabeth Meagher for Fort C. F. Smith. Mitch Buoyer and John Reeshaw, both half-breeds acted as scouts. The streams were very high, the roads almost impassable because of mud and late snow. They did not reach Fort C. F. Smith until June 10. Numerous small parties of Sioux and Crows were seen on the road but the train was not attacked. This can be accounted for, because at this time most of the Sioux were on Powder river holding sun dances and the small bands that were hanging about Fort Smith were there for the purpose of trading with the Crows for arms and ammunition, which those Indians were getting regularly from the traders north, and from Fort C. F. Smith. They did not feel strong enough to attack so large a party and were laying low preparing for the grand raid when they expected to completely

annihilate the white race.   Reeshaw and Buoyer kept
in the lead and had various talks with the Sioux which
partly accounts for their keeping at a distance.   Blackfoot, a Crow chief, joined the expedition on the Yellowstone and proceeded with them to Fort Smith, but
he left the greater portion of his band at Clark's fork.

In the midst of all these military preparations General Meagher, the leading spirit, fell from a steamboat
at Fort Benton and was drowned on July 1, 1867.

Early in July a party of Flathead Indians camped
within a few miles of Camp Meagher and stole some
horses from a nearby ranch.   Captain Campbell with
a squad went to the camp and recovered the horses and
demanded the thief.   The first night the Indian could
not be found but arrived in camp next day and the chief
at once surrendered him to the captain, who declared
his intention of hanging him; but told the chief that he
would reprieve him if he said so.   The chief said he
was a very bad Indian who gave much trouble and that
he wished him to die: so he was hung in the presence
of the camp.

Shortly after this, a party of one hundred Crows
came to the Gallatin on a horse-stealing raid.   Captain
Nelson and a companion on their way from Bozeman
to the camp were advised of the matter.   Captain
Nelson with his company, immediately started in pursuit and after a hot race for more than thirty miles they
overhauled the Indians at the ferry of the Yellowstone,
killed two and recovered the stolen stock.   The first
one killed at the ferry had braided in his hair a long
strand of light brown hair, evidently from the scalp of
some white woman recently murdered, yet these Crows
were supposed to be friendly Indians.   This Indian's

scalp was taken together with the lock of long brown hair and sent to Bozeman as a souvenir.

On October 23, 1867, the Montana militia was mustered out. The cost of the campaign was $1,100,000.00. Col. Neil Howie and Col. Chas. D. Curtis paid the Helena men in full out of their own pockets and were never reimbursed. Colonel Black of Bozeman furnished supplies generously, all of which were never paid for. Merchants and ranch men all over the state furnished horses and supplies generously, taking vouchers for pay. The legislature of 1868-69 adopted resolutions setting forth the claims of the citizens for services rendered the government during the Indian wars. These claims were considered by the general government as being excessive and no appropriation was made to pay them. In 1872, General Hardee was sent to the territory to investigate the claims and after his report Congress made an appropriation of the sum of $515,325.00 to pay the vouchers, but by this time most of the vouchers had been sold to speculators for little or nothing and the people who rendered the services as a rule received little or no remuneration.

From a very early period, if not from its beginning, our management of Indian affairs has presented a most astounding and humiliating spectacle; being a mixture of stupidity, foolish sentimentalism, utter mismanagement, and hypocritical rascality, which later came into full bloom with the advent of Grant's so called "Quaker policy," and thrived luxuriantly for many years thereafter. The Indians became wards of the government. Large areas of land (about one fourth of Montana, consisting of the choicest agriculture land in the territory) was set aside for their exclusive use and benefit. They were to be provided with schools and churches and were to be educated and taught the arts of civilization. Rations, clothing, and farming utensils were to be issued quarterly, and they were to receive large sums of money as indemnity for lands relinquished to the government. The white man was not to be allowed to come on the Indian reservation unless by permission of the agent. This all looked well on paper, but let us take a review and see how it worked out in practice.

The Indian was told that he *must* remain on his reservation, but there was no provision made to compel him to do so or to compel Congress to appropriate money to pay them for their relinquished lands. There possibly were not more than a dozen men in Congress at that time who had ever seen an Indian and not one who knew a thing about the minds or customs of the Indians of the great plains. Men from the far east were usually selected for Indian agents.

The Indians east of the Rocky mountains were fully alive to the advantages and disadvantages of treaties. Their fathers and grandfathers had made treaties with the whites. Some of the old chiefs had medals presented to them as far back as President Madison's time.

They might get the money for their relinquished lands but the chances were that they would not, and they governed themselves accordingly. Commissions composed of high dignitaries from Washington journeyed out to the Bad Lands of Dakota and Montana to make treaties with these savages. A description of one of these councils, which my brother James attended at Fort Sully, is a fair sample of all of them, and I will give it here.

In October, 1865, a commission, whose members were

Gov. George N. Edwards of Dakota, Rev. H. W. Reed, Gen. H. H. Sibley, Gen. Samuel R. Curtis, Col. E. B. Taylor, and O. Guernsey came up the river in the steamer "Calypso" ladened with goods and trinkets to be delivered in the form of presents to those who were willing to treat. This body of dignified gentlemen, representatives of our great government, waited about the fort ten days before any of the Indians appeared and then but a few bands of Sioux came in. The Cheyennes and Arapahoes refused to make any treaty whatsoever. The councils were held inside the stockades at Fort Sully and the beginning of the pow-wow was attended by much ceremony. The Indians conducted their part with much dignity.

The Indians were camped on the plains below the fort. The chiefs rode up, accompanied by an escort of young warriors mounted on their best horses and themselves and ponies decked out in all of their available savage finery with their faces and persons liberally daubed with vermilion paint. Only the chiefs and head tribesmen were allowed inside the stockade. At the gate they dismounted and strode across the open space with heads erect, never deigning to glance to right or left until they reached the council tent.

The members of the commission occupied a place at the end of the tent; behind them was the shield of the United States draped with bunting and the stars and stripes. In front of them and spread out around were the chiefs surrounded by their retinue, decked out in their robes of state which consisted of elaborately decorated feather head-dress and robes highly ornamented with beaded embroidery, quills, elk's teeth, and bits of scarlet cloth. One chief had ermine skins in number and quality to have done honor to the Czar of Russia.

The council opened by General Curtis presenting the terms of the treaty, which was for the opening of a road up the North Platte and Powder rivers along the base of the Big Horn mountains and over to the Yellowstone; the Indians were to retire to their reservation; receive rations; schools, churches, houses for their use were to be constructed, teachers, carpenters, blacksmiths and artisans were to be sent. They were to receive farm implements and be instructed in the art of farming. A large sum of money was to be paid them in ten annual payments. Emigration was to travel unmolested on this road and up the Missouri river by boat.

Iron Nation, head chief of the Brulé Sioux made answer. The Indian is a natural-born orator and Iron Nation possessed this racial trait in a very high degree. He made a speech of two hours' duration, enumerating with great force the reasons for their hostility to the white man. "You wish us to plant corn. God gave us the heavens and the earth, the buffalo and the arrows to kill them with. We kill the buffalo and our women and children have food and clothing, always we have done this; the buffalo are here always and always we have arrows. The buffalo are the Indian's cattle. God gave them to the Indians – the white man has another kind of cattle, they are not the buffalo. We do not want the white man to come with his rifles and kill our cattle. We have planted corn and the frosts kill it – we do not like to plant corn, we had rather hunt buffalo for that is sure. Our women and children are never hungry or cold when we hunt buffalo. We do not like your building forts on our land. The soldiers come with many guns, the white men trade fire water to our young men and then they have a bad heart they will not listen to the councils of the chiefs, they kill white men and then the soldiers come with the big guns and kill all – old men, women, and children – all. Can't you see? You know this. You lie when you say you do not. We will be at peace when you go away and leave us alone. You always come with lies. We show you our papers. They were given us by the big captain who swears, the white chief, with the gray beard (meaning General Harvey). You all tell lies. Tell your great chief these things." While he spoke some of the Indians showed restlessness and much animosity, but finally Iron Nation strode forward and signed the treaty, touching the pen six times one for each of the charges he had brought against the whites; then casting a withering glance at the commission he turned and left the tent.

Medicine Ball, a young chief of the Lower Brulés, was a magnificent looking fellow. When he rose to speak he stood six feet two inches in his moccasins, he was naked to the waist and presented a perfect picture of muscle and manly beauty. A highly ornamented robe was thrown carelessly over one shoulder and an unusually large number of scalps dangled from handle of a war club worn at his side, emblems of his prowess at war. He was extremely bitter in his denunciations of the whites. "What are you here for? We did not send for you, we do not want the white men to come. You say you wish to make a treaty. We are here to listen but what we shall do is another thing." This about expressed the sentiments of most of the young Indians.

White Hawk, a very old chief of the Yanktons, wore a silver medal presented to him at a treaty during President Madison's administration. He held up the silver medal and asked, "Why do you come here? You come for our land, you come always begging. The land is ours. We have given you land before."

White Hawk had parchments of four other treaties that he had signed all of which had been broken by our government. These he presented one at a time to General Sibley asking each time, "Who broke this? Who lied, white man or Indian? You speak with two tongues. Your agents are thieves. We do not want your presents. White men sell fire water to our young men that gives them bad hearts. Go! We will not plant corn, we will hunt buffalo and the deer. We will listen but our hearts are sad. My people do not want the roads built. We do not want the white man to come." For several days White Hawk refused to sign but finally came forward and touched the pen.

One old chief came forward and said, "Who is afraid to sign this paper? I will sign it with my feet and hands." And suiting the action to the word he touched the pen first with each foot and then with each hand. This was considered a very significant ceremony as the ground upon which they stand is considered by an Indian as an emblem of eternity. Doubtless the old chief intended it to mean that it was the last treaty he proposed to sign.

The council lasted two weeks when finally all the chiefs present had signed, then the peace pipe, a large pipe carved from red sandstone, on the stem of which were cut many notches, records of other treaties, was passed. This ended the pow-wow but for the next week all hands at Sully were busy distributing rations and presents to the waiting throng of Indians who seemed highly pleased with this part of the program.

The haughty young Brulé and disdainful White

Hawk were promptly on hand to receive their share of the spoils. Many thousands of dollars worth of presents were handed out to them, including ammunition and guns. The Indians took their presents and decamped. So ended this treaty, but what the result!

The rations issued to the Indians consisted of flour, beans, rice, dried fruits, syrup, sugar, coffee, and tobacco. As they had subsisted on an almost exclusive meat diet for generations, the gorging themselves with unaccustomed food made them very ill; in fact some of the children who had eaten large quantities of uncooked dried apples and had drunk syrup from the can like water, died from the effects. The Indians attributed this to poisoning and of course had an added grievance against the whites. Treaties were forgotten; guns and ammunition brought forth, tomahawk and scalping knife sharpened and as soon as the grass was green and the weather warm they again took the war path; stealing, plundering, murdering, and destroying all property within reach.

Another treaty was called, and these same Indians with scalps of women and children, victims of recent atrocities, dangling from their belts, appeared at the council. More speeches were made – more promises – more presents – more guns and ammunition issued to red-handed murderers, and all was ready for fresh outrages on defenseless settlers and unprotected travelers.

In April, 1868, another commission came to Fort Laramie to make another treaty. This Laramie treaty was the most atrocious of them all and was responsible for the continuous Indian wars and massacres which lasted until 1881. At this time Chiefs Sitting Bull and Gaul, with their bands, surrendered at Fort Yates and

were sent to Standing Rock agency; there to live at the
expense of the government, in ease and luxury. This
treaty gave to the Indians, for their exclusive use and
benefit, the territory commencing on the Missouri river
at forty-six N. latitude down east to a point opposite to
the northern line of Nebraska, then along this line to
longitude one hundred four degrees west, thence north
on a meridian line to a point where the forty-sixth
parallel intersects the same, and east along parallel
forty-six to the point at its crossing of the Missouri;
together with existing reservations on the east bank of
the Missouri. They were also to have all the country
north of the North Platte and east of the summit of the
Big Horn mountains. It further provided for the
closing of the Bozeman road to Montana, and the removal of all military posts in this ceded territory, and
further stipulated that the government should punish
white men or other Indians who perpetrated a wrong
on the tribe and to punish wrong doers among the tribe.
They received presents of food, clothing, ammunition,
firearms, knives, tomahawks, beads, paint, and trinkets.
For all this they gave nothing but their promise to be
good.

There was no possible excuse for such a treaty with
these Indians. They were not being driven from their
homes or ceding large tracts of territory to the whites.
To the contrary they were themselves interlopers. They
were Sioux who had been driven out of Minnesota in
1863 for the atrocities committed by them on the
whites; and as a reward were receiving a section of
country rich in agricultural and mining resources, as
large as the present state of Montana and were promised the protection of the United States government
against invasion from without or any internal disturb-

ance among themselves. They were furthermore to be provided with arms and ammunition, food and clothing that they might be the better prepared for their marauding parties against the white settlers and their Indian neighbors.

The forts must be abandoned that there might be nothing to interfere with their pleasant diversion of butchering defenseless white settlers and plundering and destroying their property. And this is exactly what they did.

The chiefs who were at the council and signed the treaty were on the war path in less than a fortnight and murdered the settlers with the guns and ammunition furnished them by the government. They scalped defenseless women and children with their new sharp knives and tomahawks presented to them at the conclusion of the treaty.

Now we will turn once more to the agencies. The treaties established the boundaries of the lands apportioned to each tribe and an agent (who was usually a man from the east without any knowledge whatever of Indians) sent to look after their affairs.

Schools were established and usually presided over by the wife, sister, or daughter of the agent who sat in front of empty desks and their labors consisted chiefly in making out elaborate reports and sending them to Washington. The farming machinery was hauled about to different places on the reservation and left to fall to pieces. The farming done was limited to a small garden patch grown for the exclusive use of the agent and his family and instead of the Indian being instructed in gardening he was rigidly excluded from the place by a high picket fence placed around it to keep him from stealing the vegetables when grown.

Instead of remaining near the agency the Indian kept as far away as possible. He had no intention of sending his children to school or of himself learning to farm. Indeed it would be nothing short of a miracle had he had any such an inclination. Nothing in his experience had ever caused him to feel the need of an education or of cultivating the soil. The chase supplied his every need; and horse-stealing raids and war parties to neighboring tribes furnished diversion. He had no intention of changing his happy mode of existence for one contrary to his nature and wholly distasteful to him, and there was no one to compel him to keep the treaties which he signed.

True there were armies sent out for the purpose of protecting the settlers who came in to occupy the lands thrown open for settlement; but so bound up with red tape that they were worse than useless. The inactivities of these armies only the more fully impressed the Indians with the idea that the whites were afraid of them. If an army officer took things into his own hands and attempted to punish them, as they deserved to be, for their unprovoked massacres he would at once be called to Washington and severely reprimanded if not dismissed from the service.

Whiskey traders there were in numbers who infested the reservations. Selling whiskey to the Indians was a crime attended by severe punishment if caught, but owing to the unsettled country and great distances they plied their trade in comparative safety. A goodly share of the money paid the Indian for lands found its way into the pockets of these bootleggers.

There was also the Indian ring. Many persons made huge fortunes furnishing supplies to the government for the Indians and the armies in the country. It was

CAPTURE OF WHISKEY TRADERS
From an original water-color drawing made by an old wolfer,
Andy McGown

FORT CAMPBELL IN 1865
Fort Campbell was an adobe structure built as a fur-trading post
about 1846. It was soon sold to the American Fur Company, and abandoned for Fort Benton nearby. The Jesuits used it for a time as a
mission. In 1865 it was occupied by a detachment of soldiers to protect the white settlers from the Indians. Their protection was so
feeble that William Fisk Saunders told them that if they would bring
over their arms, the settlers would protect them
From an original pencil drawing by Granville Stuart

owing largely to the influence of these unscrupulous persons that Indian affairs were conducted as they were.

A good story went the rounds in the early seventies in which there was more truth than poetry. Three gentlemen arrived in Montana from the Humboldt river country and shortly thereafter one of the trio was elected delegate to Congress and secured for his friend an Indian agency and the other member of the trio was engaged as clerk of the agency. He being a man of genius proposed a scheme for the enrichment of himself and his principal. He collected straggling Indians from different bands and tribes and founded the "Teton Sioux." The name was derived from the three beautiful mountain peaks at the head of Snake river near which the new tribe was colonized. They were represented by the agent as being the most blood-thirsty savages, who had declared a war of extermination against the whites, their number was estimated at eleven thousand. These reports properly substantiated were sent to Washington and through the instrumentality of the congressman, Mr. S—— was appointed "special agent" for the new tribe. He was supposed to have had an interview with the head chief at the risk of his life. The result of the "big talk" was sent to Washington. The Tetons were represented as being hostile and about to take the war path, but hopes were entertained that presents would keep them quiet and bring about friendly relations between them and the whites. A modest appropriation of five hundred thousand dollars was asked for this purpose. The eloquent delegate from the territory pressed the matter at Washington and a bill appropriating five hundred thousand dollars for the "Teton Sioux" became a law.

After a goodly portion of the money had been ex-

pended, not on the Indians but among the members of
the ring, rumors reached Washington that the "Teton
Sioux" really did not exist, the agent started with a
few Indians, kept up by the ring for the purpose of
making annual visits to the national capital, and arrived
there in due time. The presence of the agent and his
plumed and blanketed warriors at Washington was
enough to satisfy the most skeptical and the agent was
granted an additional ten thousand dollars to defray
the expenses of himself and charges to Washington and
return.

In 1874 Major Maginnis (our then delegate to Congress) explained to an Indian commission why it was
that the Indian appropriations were increasing at the
rate of a million dollars a year and yet the Indians were
dissatisfied and continually on the war path. He said
that he had personal knowledge of the operations of the
Indian bureau and Indian agents.

"They will take a barrel of sugar to an Indian tribe
and get a receipt for ten barrels. For a sack of flour
the Indians sign a receipt for fifty sacks. The agent
will march three hundred head of cattle four times
through a corral, get a receipt for twelve hundred head,
give a part of them to the Indians, sell part to a white
man, and steal as many back as possible."

Mr. Maginnis strongly recommended placing the
Indian affairs in the hands of army officers who would
treat the Indians with justice and firmness, and who
have no relish for Indian wars, as they entail much
hardship and bring no glory.

In 1868 Fort Shaw was built on Sun river about five
miles above the town and four companies of the 13th
infantry were stationed there to protect the settlers and
the Benton road. So frequently had the Wells, Fargo

Company coaches been fired upon and the stations raided and stock driven off by Indians that a company of mounted cavalry was ordered from Fort Shaw to patrol the road between Kennedy's ranch and Tingley's.

Early in April, 1868, the Blackfeet made their appearance in the Gallatin valley and along the Benton-Virginia City road. A party stole a bunch of stock from Nelson Storey, but was pursued and all the stolen stock recovered. Three of the animals died later from arrow wounds.

On the twenty-seventh of April, taking advantage of a dark rainy night, they entered the town of Bozeman and stole fifteen head of horses. An expedition of citizens outfitted in the morning and started out in pursuit. They were gone several days but as the Indians had several hours the start they made good their escape and the pursuers found neither Indians nor stock.

On the return to town the party found the body of Peter Cahill, on the road near Aults' mill. He had been to the coal mine for coal and was overtaken by the Blackfeet and killed and scalped. The wagon was left standing in the road but they had cut the harness into small bits and scattered it along the road. The four fine mules accompanied the Indians.

Word came to Fort Shaw that a band of Bloods was camped on the Teton and had in their possession much stolen stock. Sixty troopers under Lieutenants Newman and Stafford set out in pursuit of them. The Indians not feeling secure, hastened north and crossed the British line with their plunder. The soldiers scouted around for twelve days until their provisions were exhausted and then returned to Fort Shaw.

On May 20, 1868, a party of five Indians came down from the bluff opposite the boat landing on the Yellow-

stone and drove off eleven horses belonging to a French-
man. Soon after word reached Colonel Broadwater
that the camp of J. J. Rowe, eight miles below Benton,
had been attacked, the horses and mules driven away
and the camp plundered by a large band of Bloods.
Broadwater, accompanied by thirty-five well-armed
men, was soon in the saddle in pursuit of the marauders.
They not only rescued their own stock but recovered
a band of cattle belonging to I. G. Baker and Company.

Six days later forty Blackfeet raided the Missouri
valley and drove off two hundred head of horses and
mules. Six ranchmen and an Indian boy, who had
been raised by a white family, started in pursuit and
overtook them on Duck creek. A skirmish ensued but
the Indians so outnumbered the whites that they were
obliged to retreat. The Indian boy became separated
from his companions and was taken prisoner. The
ranchmen returned to the settlements for reinforcements. There were plenty of men who volunteered
and there were guns and ammunition but all of the
horses in the vicinity had been stolen and mounts could
not be procured for the volunteers. The Indians
crossed the Missouri river and appeared in the Deep
creek country and drove off thirty-five head of horses;
with this booty they crossed the Belt range and were
well out of reach of any but a large and well-organized
party.

On the morning of May 27 a party of seven Indians
arrived at Ivan Johnson's ranch just below Lincoln
gulch. Johnson and a hired man were in bed asleep
when their self-invited guests arrived. They opened
the door and entered without ceremony and awakened
the sleeping men and ordered them to get up and prepare breakfast. As they were taken wholly by surprise

there was nothing left for them to do but to comply. The Indians examined the contents of the cupboard, ordered the food cooked that was to their liking. While some of the party amused themselves in this way, the others took possession of the bed, there to take a smoke while awaiting the products of the frying pan. When all was ready they fell to and devoured every morsel of food in sight. They helped themselves to all the tobacco and left, taking all the horses with them. The outraged ranchers started for Lincoln gulch and twenty-five volunteers were soon in pursuit of the Indians but they were well mounted and had too much the start and so made good their escape.

A few days later a party of Piegans appeared at Confederate gulch, drove off all the horses and fired a parting shot at some miners working in a gulch just below town. These Piegans were on their return from the Missouri valley where they had committed many depredations. They had stolen horses that were picketed at the doors of houses in which families were living.

The appearance of Indians in Confederate gulch created intense excitement in Diamond City. A meeting of citizens was held and eighty men volunteered to fight Indians. A considerable sum of money and ten days provision were contributed. The women and children from the ranches were brought into Diamond City. The next day the expedition started. One division starting out in the direction of Benton, for the purpose of intercepting their retreat, while the others followed directly on their trail. This latter division came upon the Indians at the divide between the Missouri river and the Musselshell where they had a sharp skirmish. The whites were poorly armed and had but a limited amount of ammunition and were compelled to give up the fight and return to Diamond City.

The steamer "Alabama" did not leave St. Louis until the tenth of September, 1868, and her progress up stream was very slow. On the twenty-fifth of October she reached Fort Peck and, finding that she could go no farther on account of low water, discharged her cargo and tied up for the winter. X. Biedler [105] was placed in charge of the freight and a sorry time he had of it.

A large village of River Crows was camped just below the landing and they hung about; begging, stealing, and making a nuisance of themselves in general. When they were refused presents they became insolent and knocking the chinking out of the stockade amused themselves by shooting arrows at the cattle inside. There were but ten white men at Fort Peck and they were anxious to avoid trouble if possible. A wagon train was on its way from Virginia City to get the freight, and the men at the fort knew that if they had any difficulty with the Indians that they would waylay the wagon train and possibly massacre the whole party, so there was nothing to do but keep inside the stockade and put up with the annoyance until relief came, which did but from an entirely unexpected source.

On the second of November a war party of fifty Sioux put in an appearance. The Crows numbered two hundred fifty warriors and they lost no time in raiding the Sioux camp. The Sioux took refuge on a little bar on the river which was covered with a willow

---

[105] J. X. Beidler was a famous vigilante, before the establishment of courts in Montana, and after became an efficient deputy United States marshal. Judge Lyman E. Munsen in *Montana Historical Society Contributions*, vol. v (Helena, 1904) p. 210. *Ibid*, p. 283. – ED.

growth and drift wood, with a high bank in front. From this place of vantage they put up a stiff fight which lasted three days. The Crows succeeded in getting five Sioux scalps but lost one brave, whereupon they gave up the battle and returned to the fort and held a war dance just outside the stockade. The Sioux took this to be a sign that the whites had abetted the Crows and after gathering reinforcements to the number of two hundred they returned.

In the meantime, the Crows knowing that the Sioux would not be long in seeking revenge packed up and started in haste for their own country. The Sioux overtook the Crows on the Musselshell. In the encounter the Sioux lost fifteen warriors but succeeded in killing twenty-two Crows and capturing three hundred head of horses. They then returned to Fort Peck surrounded it and kept up a fight with the whites for six hours but as the men in the fort had longer range guns than the Indians they succeeded in keeping them at a safe distance.

Edgar Sears, a trapper who had been out for a couple of months, was murdered and scalped a short distance from the fort. The Sioux were led by Chief Sitting Bull who did a lot of fancy riding mounted on a splendid black horse and wearing a most gorgeous war bonnet; but was careful to keep well out of range of the rifles. The arrival of Garrison and Baird's ox train escorted by cavalry under Lieutenants Newman and Townsend put a stop to the performance. The Indians left in haste for the winter camp.

The Indian campaign of 1869 was opened when a band of ten Blackfoot Indians entered the Gallatin valley by way of the old Flathead pass, about twelve miles

northwest of Fort Ellis and proceeded to a ranch on
Dry creek where they drove off all the cattle and horses.
The alarm was given and a small party of ranchmen
went in pursuit, but fearing the Indians would soon
join a large camp and, not having sufficient ammunition
to attack a strong war party, they returned to Bozeman
for assistance.

News of the marauding party had preceded them
and forty mounted infantry men under command of
Captain Clift, accompanied by fifteen citizens had
started out on April 5 to intercept and capture them
if possible. On the third day the advance guard overtook the Indians, twelve in number, about noon. They
were on the North fork of Sixteen Mile creek, about
seventy-five miles from Bozeman. From signs discovered there were doubtless other bands of Indians in the
vicinity scattered in different directions.

On the approach of the pursuers the Indians fled to
the top of a very rough mountain, upon which was a
fortification, formed by nature, almost impregnable.
Here they imagined they were safe from the attacks
of a host, and from this point commenced shaking their
blankets at the men and making other demonstrations
of hostilities daring them to come on, cussing and
swearing in very plain English.

Captain Clift divided his forces sending Lieutenant
Thompson around the mountain upon the east. Then
came the ascent and a raking fire from the Indians.
The summit was reached at last and from the crags and
roughness of the surface they were enabled to obtain
positions that completely surrounded the Indians and
from which they could fire with safety. Nearer and
nearer the men began to close in, creeping from point

to point and firing whenever an Indian raised a gun or
made a movement. At this junction the Indians saw
that they were trapped and that there was no hope of
escape, and began singing their death song. Nearly
half of their number were killed or disabled. The
firing had been going on about two hours and the sun
was getting low; fearing that darkness would overtake
them and that the Indians would yet make their escape,
Captain Clift called for volunteers from those nearest
the fortifications to make a charge. A dozen men re-
sponded, revolver in hand and were met with fire from
the Indians. Private Conry was killed and King severely wounded but the last Indian was killed.

Such was the situation east of the Rocky mountains
and now we turn to the Indians on the other side of the
range.

That section of the country lying west of the Rocky
mountains and east of the Bitter Root range was the
home of the Salish,[106] a once numerous and powerful
tribe who had always been friendly to the whites, but
were wholly neglected by the government.

Although living west of the mountains they claimed
the headwaters of the Missouri river as their hunting
grounds and the entire tribe annually crossed the range
to hunt buffalo; only the very old people and young

---

[106] The Salish, or more generally speaking, the Flatheads were one of
the more important tribes of the Salishan family which included the Coeur
d'Alenes, the Pend' Oreille, the Kalispell, the Kootenai, the Nez Percé, and
probably the Okanogans, and other Indian tribes on the upper Columbia.
The name Salish means "we the people" and the sign was to strike the head
with the flat of the hand. Thus from this sign they apparently acquired the
name of Flathead. Father Pierre DeSmet and Father Lawrence Palladino
lived among them for many years and both express high opinions of their
character as did also Mullan and Stevens. Chittenden and Richardson
opus citra, vol. iv, pp. 1263-1265 and index. Palladino, *Indian and White
in the Northwest* pp. 1-6. – ED.

children remained at home. Their old trails across the mountains were worn deeper and had been traveled more and longer than any other Indian trails in Montana.

These hunting grounds were disputed, being claimed by the Blackfeet and from time immemorial bitter war raged between the tribes. In the earlier period of their history the Salish with their ally, the Nez Percé a small but superior tribe that lived on the upper Columbia were more than a match for the Blackfeet and hunted wherever they chose. The advent of the Hudson's Bay Company among the Blackfeet enabled that tribe to procure firearms at a much earlier period than the Salish could. This gave them such superior advantages that they not only drove the Salish from the hunting grounds but followed them across the range carrying the war into their own country and threatened to annihilate that tribe.

The Salish were not a warlike people but they wanted firearms that they might stand an equal chance in their encounters with their enemies. Firearms could only be procured from the white men, so from the first they welcomed the few trappers and traders that found their way into the Salish country.

In 1853 Isaac I. Stevens [107] on his way from St. Paul to the coast with a surveying party looking out a route for the Northern Pacific railroad came into their country and was welcomed by the chiefs and head men of the tribe. Stevens did not promise them firearms but held out the prospects of making a treaty with the

[107] Isaac Ingalls Stevens became governor of Washington Territory and superintendent of Indian affairs. He also had a leading part in the construction of the Mullan road. His life is by his son Hazard Stevens (New York, 1900, 2 vols). – ED.

Blackfeet so that both the whites and Indians could dwell in peace. This was a welcome piece of intelligence to the Salish for they were heartily tired of the never-ending wars in which they were continually worsted.

In 1855 Governor Stevens returned to the country to make a treaty with them and was accorded a hearty welcome. More than one thousand warriors arrayed in all their savage splendor rode forth to meet him. The council [108] was opened by Governor Stevens setting forth the terms offered by the government. The Indians were asked to cede extensive tracts of land, practically all that they had, and to retire to a reservation. In return they were to receive certain annuities, cattle, farming implements, seed grain; and schools were to be provided for their children. Teachers, farmers, carpenters, and blacksmiths would be sent to teach them to till the soil and to build houses.

The Indians were willing to cede the land and they did not object to the reservation plan but the location of the reservation was the stumbling block. They were in reality one tribe, the Salish but there were three branches, each inhabiting a particular section of country to which they were strongly attached. Chief Michael lived with the Kootenais on the headwaters of the Columbia and north of Flathead lake, Alexander with the Pend d'Oreilles were south of the lake and in the Jocko valley while Victor, chief of the Flatheads and hereditary chief over all, claimed for his home the beautiful valley of the Bitter Root and neither chief

[108] Council grove near the junction of the Bitter Root and Clark's fork rivers. This is an excellent account of the council. The text of the treaty is in Charles J. Kappler, editor, *Indian Affairs, Laws and Treaties* (Washington, 1903) pp. 542-545. – ED.

was willing to leave his home. The council dragged along for days without reaching an agreement and then the treaty was finally signed without settling the question of the location of the reservation.

A few presents of red paint, beads, bright calico, knives, and blankets were distributed and Governor Stevens departed. Years passed and nothing more was heard of the treaty. No cattle, farming implements, or seed grain arrived, nor farmers to teach the Indians how to till the soil.

The Salish crossed the range and hunted buffalo for their living and carried on the same old wars with the Blackfeet, and their children had no school other than those furnished by the Jesuit Fathers and Sisters of Charity that were among them when Stevens came. White people came and were welcomed and given land by the Indians until the Bitter Root valley was quite well settled and there were two good-sized towns, Stevensville and Corvallis. The old chiefs were dead and their sons reigned instead.

The white settlers begun to clamor for government titles to their lands and they wanted roads and bridges and schools. In 1871 like a bolt of thunder from a clear sky, came an order from the President to remove the Flathead Indians from the Bitter Root valley to the valley of the Jocko.

Without a shadow of right or justice and without warning or provocation these kindly peaceable Indians were to be driven from the home that had been theirs since the beginning of time. Charlot, their head chief, refused to go. In 1872 General Garfield was sent out to make a treaty with them and to try to induce them to go to the Jocko. Charlot, head chief, and Arlee and

Adolph, sub chiefs met at the council. Charlot spoke for the Indians. He remembered the treaty and he also remembered that the white men had not kept their word and the Indians could not keep theirs. He pointed out that the white people's farms were all over the Indian's hunting grounds and that the Salish still crossed the mountains and fought with the Blackfeet in order to get food and shelter and clothing. The white men or their fields had never been hurt by the Flathead Indians.

Victor, his father, said they would remain in the land of their fathers and Charlot would not go.[109] He left the council. Later Adolph and Arlee signed the treaty. Gov. B. F. Potts, Congressman William H. Claggett, Wilbur F. Sanders, J. S. Vial, and D. J. Swain signed as witnesses. General Garfield returned to Washington and the treaty was published as having been signed by all the Indians and at the same time Arlee was recognized by the government as head chief of the Flatheads. In reality Arlee was only a half-blood Flathead his father being a Nez Percé. Preparations were hurried forward for the removal of the Indians to the Jocko.

Chief Charlot was a Christian, having embraced the Catholic faith and was honest, just, and truthful in all of his dealings with the whites and had many staunch friends among the settlers in the valley. When he learned of these outrages his indignation knew no bounds, every vestige of confidence that he had had in the white race vanished, his sense of honor and justice was outraged. He declared that he would never leave the Bitter Root valley alive.

[109] Major John Owen in his Journals expressed the opinion that the Flatheads would never leave the Bitter Root unless forced to do so. – ED.

Arlee and his following moved but Charlot and his people remained. Those that went to the Jocko received something in the way of annuities but they had, to say the least, inefficient agents and but little was done to better their condition and they fared but little better than those that remained in the Bitter Root and received nothing from the government. They all continued to go to the buffalo country to hunt in order to live.

In 1877 Major Peter Ronan a man who was conversant with Indian customs and habits and of fine executive ability as well as of unimpeachable integrity was appointed agent for the Flatheads, and immediately set to work to straighten out the tangled affairs. Honest and just in all of his dealings with them he soon won their confidence and remained until his death their trusted friend and adviser. Major Ronan was familiar with the Stevens treaty and with the subsequent proceedings. His sympathies were with Charlot but he could see the futility of further resistance and used all of his powers of persuasion to induce the old chief to reconsider his decision. Charlot would not listen, his confidence in government officials was gone.

Settlers continued to pour into the valley and settled on the land. The buffalo were fast disappearing on the ranges and there was but little game in the Bitter Root and the condition of the Indians became desperate; the matter was finally taken to Congress and Senator George Vest of Missouri and Major Maginnis, our delegate in Congress, were appointed to investigate the matter. The investigation brought to light a long story of injustice, ingratitude, duplicity, and an utter disregard of treaty pledges on the part of the government agents in dealing with these Indians and their report to Washington was to that effect.   General Garfield was forced to acknowledge that Charlot had not signed the treaty.

In January, 1884, Major Ronan received instructions to bring Charlot and his head men to Washington for a conference; the object being to try to secure Charlot's consent to remove with his band to the Jocko reservation.

Nearly a month was spent in Washington and several interviews held with the Secretary of the Interior but no offer of pecuniary reward or persuasion of the secretary could shake Charlot's resolution to remain in the Bitter Root valley.   He treated with disdain and distrust any person connected with the United States government and refused all offers of assistance from the government.   He asked only the poor privilege of remaining in the valley where he was born.   In March, 1884, Major Ronan held another council at Stevensville with the Indians at which he promised: first – a choice of one hundred and sixty acres, unoccupied land on the Jocko reservation; second – assistance in erecting a substantial house; third – assistance in fencing and ploughing a field of ten acres; fourth – the following gifts; two cows to each family, a wagon and harness and necessary agricultural implements, seed for the first year and provisions until the first year's harvest. Twenty-one families accepted this offer and went to the Jocko.

The department kept its part of this contract and also authorized the construction of an irrigation ditch to cover the land settled upon.   So well did this plan work that in a year, other Indians, witnessing the prosperous condition of their friends and relatives also determined to go to the Jocko and eleven more families moved down. But alas! The red tape was in full operation again. Although Major Ronan wrote and urged and explained and finally went to Washington at his own expense to try to get the necessary funds to supply these eleven families with the things given the first twenty it was all to no purpose. The excuse given was no appropriation at that time. Later orders came to issue supplies to Charlot and those at Stevensville and again the eleven families were left out as they were not at Stevensville. Major Ronan issued them supplies assuming the responsibility himself.

Food, seed grain, and a limited amount of farming implements were issued to Charlot's little band at Stevensville; but the Indians were not farmers and they were too far away to receive instructions and supervision necessary to make their efforts a success. The young men were fast becoming addicted to the use of whiskey and the women and children were starving.

In 1891 General Carrington was sent out to see if he could make some sort of treaty whereby the Indians would remove to the Jocko. Charlot was ready to go. He said, "I do not want your land, You are liars. I do not believe you. My young men have no place to hunt, they get whiskey, they are bad. My women and children are hungry: I will go." Into exile went this truly noble Indian.

During all these years of the treating and wrangling with the Flathead Indians, the settlers in the Bitter Root valley were kept in suspense as to the titles to their lands. There was no incentive to make improvements as they did not know whether they might remain and get title or be ordered off to seek homes in some other locality.

Such was the peace policy of the government which was in operation for so many years, during which time the Indians were almost exterminated, the lives of hundreds of white people sacrificed, expensive Indian campaigns carried on, and much valuable property destroyed. A number of Indian agents and traders made fortunes, hied themselves to their eastern homes and spread stories about the murderous capacity of the white settlers who encroached upon the Indians.

Looking for a Cattle Range

In 1850 Capt. Richard Grant with his sons John and James Grant begun trading along the Emigrant road in Utah for footsore and worn-out cattle and horses. This stock was usually of good quality and only needed rest and a little care to make them fine animals.

The Grants spent the summers along the Emigrant road between Bridger and Salt Lake, and in the fall drove their stock up into what is now Montana.

In 1856 Robert Dempsey, John M. Jacobs, Robert Hereford, and Jacob Meek begun trading along the Emigrant road and drove six hundred head of cattle and horses up into Montana and they, together with the Grants, wintered on the Stinkingwater.

When we came to Montana in 1858 the Grants and Jacobs had herds of several hundred cattle and horses. These cattle fattened on the native grasses, without shelter other than that afforded by the willows, alders, and tall rye grass along the streams. In the spring they were fat and fit for beef and were driven back to the Emigrant road and traded for more footsore and worn-out animals which in turn were driven back to winter range in Montana, the favorite places being the Beaverhead, Stinkingwater, and Deer Lodge valleys.

In the fall of 1860 we drove in sixty head of cattle and Robert Hereford brought in seventy-five head from the Emigrant road. At this time there was a small herd at St. Ignatius, a few at Fort Owen, and about two hundred head in and near Fort Benton.

These herds all increased rapidly and when gold was struck at Alder gulch every emigrant train brought in a few cattle, ranches were established and by 1863 cattle growing had become an industry of considerable importance.

In 1864 a bill was introduced in the legislature regulating marks and brands. The act concerning marks and brands became a law Jan. 31, 1865.

Nelson Storey of Bozeman drove the first herd of Texas cattle into Montana in the spring of 1866. Storey purchased six hundred head of cattle at Dallas, Texas, and started north with them, arriving in the Gallatin valley on December 3 and camped where Fort Ellis was later located.

In 1878 D. S. G. Flowerree purchased one thousand head of stock cattle in Oregon and placed them on the Sun river range and then begun the stocking of ranges on a large scale.

The first beef cattle driven out of Montana was a small herd belonging to D. J. Hagan of Sun river. Hagan sold them to Ornstein and Popper and delivered them at Salt Lake City in the fall of 1866. That same fall Jerry Mann drove one hundred and thirty head of steers and fat dry cows to Ogden and sold them.

In May, 1874, James Forbis purchased three hundred head of fat beef steers from Conrad Kohrs and drove them to Ogden and from there shipped them to Omaha by rail. Later in the summer Allen drove five hundred choice steers from the Madison valley to Granger on the Union Pacific and shipped them by rail to Chicago. In the summer of 1876 Kohrs drove three hundred head of choice steers to Cheyenne, Wyoming and shipped them to Davenport, Iowa.

During the summer of 1879 a co-partnership was entered into between A. J. Davis of Butte, Erwin Davis of New York City, Samuel A. Hauser, and Granville Stuart of Helena, Montana, for the purpose of engaging in the business of cattle raising. The capital stock of the firm was one hundred fifty thousand dollars. The brand was "H." The firm name Davis, Hauser and Co. The interests were divided into thirds; the Davis Brothers one-third, Hauser one-third, and Stuart one-third. I was elected superintendent and general manager and directed to begin at once to look about for stock cattle that could be purchased at a satisfactory price.

By the first of January I had contracts for about two thousand head that could be purchased in Montana and Oregon. The price paid ranged from $14 to $17 per head according to the number of steers in the bunch. The young calves were thrown in with the mothers. By the first of March I had contracted an additional two thousand head of Oregon cattle.

SUNDAY, April 11, 1880. Left Helena for a trip to the Yellowstone country to look for a good cattle range. The first part of the journey was by stage coach.

Morning bright and pleasant, thermometer at 7 A. M. 42°, gentle breeze, Bar. 25.825. Pretty good grass on Spokane creek and on Beaver creek divide, road muddy and bad from Half-way house to Beaver creek, and then that infernal rocky road extending nearly to Bedford shook us up horribly. That is the rockiest road on this earth. Had a good dinner at Bedford and was all shaken down so that I enjoyed it.

Saw the abandoned mining town of "Hog Em" in the distance and reached Radersburg about 4 P. M.

Very little grass from Beaver creek on but in the red shale hills there are immense quantities of Mexican bayonet.

12th. Left Radersburg at 7 A. M. for Bozeman, fine range to Galen's but badly eaten out and no water obtainable for irrigation although it is all fine farming land. Good grass from near Galen's to near the Jefferson river but no water obtainable or it would be eaten out. Very strong wind today. Took dinner at West Gallatin; here saw the first faint tinge of green in the little sage along the road. Plenty of snow drifts along the fences and banks as we neared Bozeman and the mud was deep and sticky, making progress slow. The foot-hills full of big snow drifts clear down into the valley and edge of town. A different soil here extending across the mountains and down the other side to near the Yellowstone river. Black loam over hills and all and a much damper climate.

13th. Left Bozeman at 4 A. M. in a snow storm with high cold wind, when partly up the range it turned to a regular old-fashioned state's sleet, the first I ever saw in Montana. Coated twigs and grass with ice one-eighth inch thick and our clothing also. The stage was a little open spring wagon and one played-out team. We had to walk, most of the way to keep from freezing. The team mired in the snow in the sage and had to be dug out, wagon unloaded and pulled out by hitching a long rope to the tongue and then all hands pull. There were fortunately no women in the party so we all helped the stage driver to swear. Each time we mired down we all got wet to our hips and our trousers froze stiff so that we could hardly walk. Crossed the summit at an altitude of six thousand two hundred and six feet.

The sleet turned to snow when we reached the Yellowstone with a bitter N. E. wind that nearly "peeled the bark" all the rest of the day and all night. At Sweet Grass creek we changed horses and had a better team but the driver missed the road and we wandered around on an old wood road half the night tired and wet and half frozen.

It quit snowing about sunrise when we were between White Beaver and Stillwater. Confound night traveling – don't let me see but about half the country. What little I could see of White Beaver basin after it came daylight, showed that it was a pretty grass country surrounded on all sides except the N., with rocky hills covered with yellow pine woods. It lies at a considerable elevation above the Yellowstone river and about six miles from it, with a high pine ridge between, through which it breaks near the S. E. side of the basin. Plenty of old snow drifts in it and the storm has put about two and one-half inches of new snow all over it. It would be a good range for a few thousand cattle. Saw a few cattle and they looked well, as was also the case on the Yellowstone bottom to Stillwater. River runs in quite a cañon five or six hundred feet below the general level of the country on each side with small bottom on either side alternately. Nice little bottom at Keiser creek, but the prettiest that I saw, albeit it was small, was at Henslup, a short distance above Young's point where begins the famous Clark's fork bottom on the N. side of the river and the largest on the whole river.

This bottom consists of a low bottom from one to three miles wide along the river and then a bench some twenty-five or thirty feet above it which extends back

to the bluffs which are ten to twelve miles back and
thinly timbered. Saw some considerable gravel
patches along the road on the lower bottom but was told
that most of the valley was good soil if water was only
obtainable for irrigation. It is well grassed. Laid
over here to sleep and rest and had to wait until next
coach came along at 4 P. M. of the fifteenth. Have
seen no country yet where I would like to trust more
than a few thousand cattle.

At Coulson I met my old friend P. W. McAdow
who was with us at Gold creek in 1862. We had a
great old visit and enjoyed reminiscing over old times.
Coulson is a tough little town. They tell me that there
are sixteen graves on the hill above town and every one
of the occupants met a violent death.

Left Coulson at 4:15 P. M. on the fifteenth in a big
open dead axle wagon. Went down ten miles to Huntley and crossed the river on a wire ferry and took to
the high prairie about dark, for Fort Custer forty-five
miles distant. Crossed Pryors' creek soon after starting and then over high rolling prairies all night. The
driver said it was a good grass and stock region. I was
obliged to take his word for it, for it was as dark as
Ebras.

Reached Fort Custer at sunrise on the sixteenth. It
is situated on the high point between the Big and Little
Horn rivers, and about one hundred feet above them.
Elevation opposite Fort Custer 3260 feet. No settlements here, nothing but the fort because it is a part of
the Crow Indian reservation.

The valley on west side of Big Horn river is from
three to five miles wide, well grassed and with grassy
bluffs back but no water at all except in the river.

Generally good soil, very little valley land on east side of Big Horn, from Custer down to the mouth some forty miles. Green grass about two inches high from Stillwater to Huntley and about three inches high here. Had to keep to the big dead axle wagon down to Terry's landing on the Yellowstone about four or five miles above the mouth of Big Horn. Here we changed for a covered jirky.

Not a very inviting country about Terry's landing, greasewood bottoms and bluffs on north side of river runs in close to the river. Pease's bottom begins on the N. side about two miles below the mouth of Big Horn river, is rather narrow, from one-half to one and one-half miles wide and about three miles long, is bounded on N. by high cliffy bluffs. It is very fertile, sheltered from all winds and is nicely timbered with cottonwoods and some cedars and pines on the bluffs. I like it better for farming than any place that I have seen over here. Night set in before we left it and when daylight came we were just below Big Porcupine creek and in sight of Porcupine Butte, a square tower of rock on top of a conical hill some miles back from the river.

Crossed Little Porcupine in the forenoon. Both these streams have very deep beds of good size with only a small stream now but the drift wood shows that at times they overflow the bottoms on either side and become impassable torrents for days at a time. Breakfasted at Short creek if one could call boiled beans and Worcestershire sauce breakfast. Provisions all out here. Elevation 2736 feet.

We had dinner at Bull creek, a fine dinner, bread, buffalo tongue, and coffee. Arrived in Miles City about 5 P. M. April 17.

From the Porcupine clear to Miles City the bottoms are liberally sprinkled with the carcasses of dead buffalo. In many places they lie thick on the ground, fat and the meat not yet spoiled, all murdered for their hides which are piled like cord wood all along the way. 'Tis an awful sight. Such a waste of the finest meat in the world! Probably ten thousand buffalo have been killed in this vicinity this winter. Slaughtering the buffalo is a government measure to subjugate the Indians.

Passed the mouth of Rosebud river (which comes into the Yellowstone on the south side) just after crossing Little Porcupine creek. The country around the mouth of the Rosebud is low and looks better grassed than any that I have seen since I left White Beaver basin but after passing it the country soon begins to put on a sterile brown bad land appearance which grows more desolate looking all the way to Miles City (forty miles).

Tongue river is considerably larger than Sun river but is muddy like the Missouri as are all the streams here, including the Yellowstone, which is here about one hundred seventy-five yards wide now and has just become unfordable. It is about three hundred yards wide when high.

Miles City stands on the east bank of Tongue river and in a grove of big cottonwood trees of which a great many have the bark torn from the upper side of them for several feet above the ground by an ice gorge here apparently about twelve or fifteen years ago, perhaps longer: so some day the town will likely be destroyed by another gorge – bad location.

There is a wire rope ferry across the Yellowstone river about two miles above Miles City and it takes the

soldiers a long time to get a boat across.   There is also
a wire rope ferry across Tongue river at Miles City,
but both rivers are unfordable, which is very unusual
at this time of the year.

I put up with my old friend Thomas H. Irvine and
we boarded at the jail with Sheriff W. H. Bullard and
deputy Jack Johnson and jailor Wash Kelly.   Mr.
Creighton was the cook.   The hotel accommodations
in Miles City in 1880 were not first class, in fact I do
not think there were any hotel accommodations.   The
people that frequented Miles City in those days usually
came to town to stay up nights and see the sights.   They
did not feel the necessity for a bed or much to eat.
They were just thirsty.

At Miles City I outfitted with saddle horses.   Bought
two little plugs of horses for $50 each, a saddle for
$35.00, bridle $3.50, three halters $1.50 each, four sad-
dle blankets $12.

Thomas Irvine had a good saddle horse and a pack
mule with two pack saddles.   I induced him to accompany me on the trip.

Waited until the twenty-second for Captain Baldwin
to return from Fort Custer as he was desirous of going
with us on the trip but the Cheyenne Indians started a
racket and he could not go.   He loaned us a good army
tent.

Left Miles City on the twenty-second at 11 A. M. and
went up the river twenty-three miles to Anderson's
ranch where we fell in with Yellowstone Kelley
(Luther S. Kelley) Phillips, Eugene Lamphere, a
nephew of Captain Baldwin, an L. A. Huffman, a
young photographer [110] from Fort Keogh.   They were

[110] Mr. Huffman is still living at Miles City.   He has photographed much
of the life of the country around. – ED.

looking for timber fit for lumber and for a small cattle range.

It sprinkled rain all day and looked very threatening. We did not put up our tent but all slept in the cabin on the hardest dirt floor that I ever laid down on.

APRIL 23.   Packed up at 7 A. M. and started in a drizzling rain.   Tom Irvine's pony objected and lit in to buck and frightened the pack mule and he lit out across the hills with the entire party in pursuit. Rounded him up and brought him back to the road. By this time it was raining hard and continued so until about 11 A. M. when it turned into a snow storm which fell fast with a high wind.   We kept on to Smith's ranch, three miles below the mouth of the Rosebud and camped with George Johnson and Ed Maguire who we found there storm bound.   They were short of provisions but we had a good supply and the cabin was large enough to hold us all.   There was a big fireplace and plenty of wood.   We each took turns cooking.   Smith had just built a large new house which he was using temporarily as a stable and into which we put most of our horses and fed them hay.   It snowed furiously all afternoon and all night and was bitter cold.

Plenty of big scrubby ash trees in the breaks along the dry creeks and bluffs and also many short ravines full of rather nice cedar trees.   Excellent grass everywhere but it is rotten now.   Green grass is about three to four inches high.   Saw many antelope and the boys shot at them several times.   Kelley finally bagged one and we had fresh meat for supper.   Traveled but fifteen miles this day.

APRIL 24.   Snowed all night and still snowing and

badly drifted, and bitter cold. Laid up in Smith's cabin all day. Only nine of us in one small cabin. This is a horrible spell of weather, kept our horses in the house and fed them hay. A flock of black birds are in a tree and some of them singing.

APRIL 25. As it seemed to have cleared up we packed up and started. There were six inches of snow on the level and drifts two and one-half feet deep. Traveled three miles up the Rosebud and here lived a solitary man, Joe McGee. At this point we separated. "Yellowstone" Kelley and Phillips went across the hills west of the Rosebud to look for pine timber and we kept on up the Rosebud twenty-two miles, having much trouble getting through the snow drifts on the edge of coulees. Killed a buck antelope but the meat was not good. From this up it is a sage country with some good grass but badly broken bad lands. Poor range and no water except in the rivers and it is a detestable mean stream to water stock. Deep narrow channel, with steep muddy banks, water very muddy and deep with miry bottom. Came near swimming and miring to get across it and there are very few places where it is possible to cross at all. The roads are very muddy and traveling slow and laborious and hard on the horses. We camped in a muddy bottom where the buffalo had eaten off most of the grass. From the bluff the Little and Big Wolf mountains are both in sight far to the south. Traveled twenty-five miles this day.

APRIL 26. Started from camp at 7:30 A. M., traveled thirteen miles and camped just above the Cone butte at the end of Little Wolf mountains on the east side of Rosebud. Fine bottom land well grassed, a good deal of black ash and box elder along the river but it is the same muddy miry stream as below. At this point the country opens out into more of a valley. Hills are low and grassy, with many cañons and beautiful buttes with scattering yellow pine timber. This open grassy valley is about one mile wide and probably eighteen miles long with little grassy vales running far back among picturesque buttes. The Big Wolf mountains are heavily timbered and perfectly white with this last snow.

If there was any other water (which there is not permanently) than in the Rosebud or if it were a different kind of stream this would be a good range for one thousand to fifteen hundred cattle but as it is it wouldn't do at all for they would all mire in the Rosebud.

Just before camping time I discovered a band of buffalo bulls up a little draw to the south and Huffman and I went and killed one. We took the tongue, the tenderloin, and the "fries." Huffman considered them a great delicacy. I preferred the loin fried in a separate pan with strips of bacon. The others of the party going to camp killed a white-tailed deer. There was a band of buffalo, about fifty in number, across the river from camp but we did not trouble them.

Traveled twenty-eight miles this day, roads muddy in places but the snow nearly all gone in the low lands.

APRIL 27. Had to mend a broken pack saddle which kept us in camp until nine o'clock. Buffalo all around us. Huffman and Eugene couldn't resist the temptation to have a run so they crossed the Rosebud and went for a bunch that was grazing along the edge of a ridge and after a lively chase across the bench land killed one. Only took the tongue as we had all the fresh meat that we could use.

The country is very beautiful although the valley is narrow. We are passing through what is called the cañon where the Rosebud cuts through the Big Wolf mountains, but it is not much of a cañon, being never less than one mile wide and with beautiful little grassy vales extending back among the picturesque castilated red buttes which have considerable nice yellow pine scattered over them. Went twelve miles and camped for noon, rested until 2 P. M. and then traveled on ten miles and camped at 5 P. M. because it looked like rain. During this ten miles we passed two nice creeks coming in from the southeast with beautiful little valleys along them, extending back as far as we could see but they were mud bottomed and steep miry banks, although their waters are almost clear, while Rosebud is still thick with mud and has a yellowish brick dust color and deposits a thick layer of mud in the buckets of water left standing a few minutes.

The scenery these ten miles is very beautiful, buttes and bastioned fortresses of all shapes and sizes capped and often landed with broad belts of vivid red scoviacious shelly rock, crowned with beautiful clumps of yellow pine trees and in many of the glades and sags are fine groves which add much to the beauty of the scene and where burned off, the hills are green with new grass. It is all a scene of beauty and only the river is vile. This day's travel was through a good grazing country where plenty of hay could be cut all along, but there is no accessible water and therefore it won't do for cattle. Hundreds of buffalo in sight all the time. We had lots of fun running them but had to forego much of the pleasure as the sport is too much for our horses.

Traveled twenty-two miles this day. The bottoms

were heavily timbered with good black ash and box
elder, till the last five miles, when the timber began to
run out. Valley along here about one-half mile wide
with little lateral valleys extending back into hills
which are becoming more grassy on their sides and
summits. Passed several streams coming in from
northwest side which looked as though they might be
permanent ones, and camped opposite one of considerable size. Put up our tent for the first time and just at
dark it began to rain slowly.

WEDNESDAY, April 28. Rained hard in the early
part of the night and was very lowering and threatening this morning with light showers of rain and snow.
Waited to see if it would clear up so did not leave camp
until 11 A. M. It was still cloudy with a cold northwest wind. Traveled up the Rosebud six miles.
Country all burned over last fall but it is a fine grass
region, much resembling some parts of high prairies in
Iowa, with small groves of ash and box elder in ravines
and along little creeks which are mostly dry now, and
have mud beds. The valley of the Rosebud here opens
out into a sort of basin; hills low and grassed all over –
high snowy hills to the southwest in the fork of the
creek. The whole country is black with buffalo.
Eugene killed one. Being a boy he couldn't resist killing just one, although we did not need the meat. He
took the tongue. Came to a dry creek which came in
from the S. E. and as a very large and old trail went up
it I knew that it must be the Indian trail crossing over
to Tongue river so we followed it for about ten miles
to the top of the divide and then a couple of miles further where we camped on a beautiful clear little creek
with fish in it, which proved to be a tributary of

Tongue river. Some ash and box elders even up here (elevation 4056 feet). The country is now all broken up into low grassy hills and mounds. No timber but splendid grass everywhere and buffalo in every direction. This high region is about one-third covered with hugh snow drifts left by the storms of the twenty-third and twenty-fourth. It froze ice one-half inch thick in this camp. We all went fishing and caught about a dozen small ones that we fried for supper. Altitude at camp 4056 feet. Traveled sixteen miles this day.

APRIL 29. Traveled southeast a few miles and struck another small tributary of Tongue river through a good grass region though broken. Some nice pine timber in clumps and many scattering yellow pines. Run out of snow banks some time before reaching the river. Saw four black-tailed deer, first on the trip. Small bands of buffalo in sight all the way down to Tongue river, which we struck in the cañon at upper edge of Wolf mountains. River quite muddy here. Curious firey red cliffs, bluffs, and buttes, evidently caused by the burning out of great beds of lignite and oily shales which once underlaid all this region. There are indications of petroleum all along from the Porcupine to here. Tongue river is about the size of Sun river and is quite low and can be forded on any riffle.

After we rested and had dinner, Eugene Lamphere and L. A. Huffman packed up and started down the river on their return to Fort Keogh and Tom and I are left alone. We miss our friends sadly. Eugene has all the enthusiasm of a boy of twenty-one, in a country where everything is new and wonderful to him, and Huffman is one of the most companionable men I ever traveled with. Tom Irvine is the best reconteur on earth and we have had some great old times on this trip. This morning Irvine's little roan objected to being saddled in the cold and wet and bucked into the campfire, scattering coffee-pot and frying pans, consequently we had plenty of ashes for relish.

APRIL 30, 1880. Started at 7 A. M. and traveled up Tongue river. Saw ten white-tailed deer soon after we left camp but did not get a shot. The white-tailed deer is the hardest game in America to get a shot at. Both hearing and scent are peculiarly sensitive. An old Indian friend of mine sizes up the situation in this way:

"Wild turkey hard to kill. Indian break some stick, turkey stop one second, say maybe Injin, Injin be good hunter he get shot. White-tailed deer, he hear some little noise way off – say Injin by God! W-u-zz he gone, Injin no get one shot."

That is about the way it is. White-tailed deer hear or scent a hunter before he gets in gunshot and they are off in an instant.

We followed up Tongue river twenty-four miles and crossed the river twenty times, it being the crookedest stream in Montana, with long high spurs or points of mountains putting down into every bend with considerable bottom-land which was well grassed but often mixed with tall young sage. Only tolerable grass on spurs and hills. At about eighteen miles we emerged from the upper end of the cañon into a high rolling country, pretty well grassed with a good deal of sage on bottoms and on hills, and many high rather rocky buttes in sight and scattered about, with a few pines and plenty of big black ash and box elder and some small groves of cottonwood. Not a very inviting looking country, has a sombre red and brown appearance and is not a good stock region. Too rocky and too much sage which holds the snow and does not allow it to drift or blow away. Irvine killed a goose, flying, with his Winchester this A. M. Dense growth of scrub cedar on most of the mountain sides, with a few yellow pines in the cañons. Elevation here 3356 feet. Traveled twenty-four miles this day.

MAY 1, 1880. Traveled thirteen miles and camped at the mouth of Prairie Dog creek. Elevation 3356 feet. This creek is about fifteen to twenty feet wide and a good swift current and is very muddy. It comes in from the south. Country not so good. Since the first five miles too much sage and rocky hills and burnt looking country and no water, excepting in Tongue river and Prairie Dog creek. Here we found a nice little white and dun spotted horse, doubtless dropped by Sioux Indians as they came through here to steal horses from the Crows.

We only traveled eight miles in the afternoon and camped across the river from two new hewed log houses that had been built last winter. Nobody at the houses. Large good grassed bottom along here but a good deal of sage among it and much short sage on the rusty looking hills. Mired our pack mule down in crossing a coulee near river, but after two hours of hard work we got him out and our stuff carried out on the dry ground. All the coulees are miry near the mouth and so is the river and deep when still, but fordable on all ripples. Quite a creek comes in here from the west, very muddy with deep cut banks and could not cross it. Had to cross the river below its mouth. Hardly a pine or a cedar along route today. I killed a fine fat goose today, and we roasted it on a spit over our camp fire.

MAY 2. Traveled twelve miles and camped for noon about one and one-half miles above the mouth of Goose creek which comes in from the southeast. It is nearly clear and is about two-thirds as large as Tongue river above the junction, the latter still quite muddy. Plenty of black ash and box elder all along the river and some nice small cottonwood groves. Very heavy growth of grass on bottoms which are not very large, but not very good on brown rocky burnt hills. Too much sage on both bottoms and hills. No old big sage but a young slim tall growth. No good country so far for stock. Found a bench where the grass had been burned off and where the young grass was very forward, being about three to four inches high. We let our poor horses fill up well on this grass at noon.

Saw many white-tailed deer today but they are all wild. Irvine killed a yearling just before we camped. Took the hams which are nice and tender. Saw five black-tailed deer on a hill. One buck had beautiful antlers but we did not have time to go after them. Passed several creeks on the north side of the river that have plenty of timber on them and camped on a clear rocky-bottomed creek, about a mile below an un-occupied cabin near which was a bay horse. A few miles before camping the sage ran out and the hills and valley are covered with a good growth of buffalo and gramma grass. This grassy belt is only about six to eight miles wide from foot of mountains out and then runs into the brown burnt somber-tinted hills and bluffs covered with short sage among which is some good bunch grass and the country rather rough and rocky.

The greatest objection to this for a cattle country is that nearly all the streams have steep-cut banks and deep channels and it is very hard to find a place where they can be crossed and especially where a place to get down and out is found, the bottom of the stream and both edges are usually miry and the coulees are miry when the snow is going off and after rains.

Elevation five miles below the Bozeman road 3906 feet and at the Bozeman road 4000 feet. Traveled twenty-five miles this day.

MAY 3.   Started at 7:30 A. M. went up Tongue river three miles and came to the stage station of the mail route from the U. P. R. R. at Rock creek to Fort Custer [111] via Reno and Fort McKinney.   At this point were three men trying to plow in the bottom with two mules and two horses all abreast.   Asked them some questions about snow fall, etc.   The chap that stammered and choked made himself spokesman much to our annoyance.   He said there was a foot of snow and it went off and came on again and went off and sometimes they had snow and sometimes not any and it was warm winds in spells and then the wind was cold and then there was more snow and a warm wind and "you know how it is around here pretty much all the time." They had a herd of one hundred thirty cattle and nine of them died.

Elevation at this point 4000 feet.   Here were several

[111] Fort Custer was established in 1877 on the Big Horn river not far from the battle ground of Custer's last fight to hold the Crow Indians in check. Its establishment came as a result of the Custer battle. Hubert Howe Bancroft, History of Montana in *Works*, vol. xxxi (San Francisco, 1890) p. 719. Fort Reno on Powder river was built in 1865 to protect the Bozeman trail. It was abandoned in 1868 as a result of the Fetterman massacre. For history see Hebard and Brininstool *opus citra*, vol. ii, pp. 122-135. Fort McKinney was on Piney fork of Powder river near the present site of Buffalo, Wyoming. *Ibid.*, vol. i, p. 255 – ED.

cabins and a bridge across the river and a woman with five very small children. They must have been twins and triplets they were all so near one size. They also had some hogs and chickens.

Went up to the foot of the mountains and took the old Bozeman road but before we reached it we came to a creek with very muddy water and utterly impassable steep banks. Could get neither in nor out and had to go two miles below where there was an abandoned ranch. Someone had dug down the banks and made a crossing. These steep-banked miry streams would be bad for cattle.

The Big Horn mountains have upheaved the strata which all slope down toward the plains and this grassy belt from six to eight miles wide along the base is evidently owing to the erosion of a vast quantity of these tilted strata which were softer and which has given to the country along the foot of the mountains a smooth and rounded look with a more fertile soil generally.

Cloud peak which has been in full view since we crossed the divide coming from Rosebud is really a very lofty point. It is a sort of jagged ridge or crest with a number of craggy peaks on it, and from it, west, for more than forty miles the top of the range is above timber line. From there west it gradually slopes down till just west of the Big Horn cañon it is quite low.

These mountains are very steep all along this side and are poorly timbered with scrubby trees – at least until high up on them where it may be better. There is no timber in the foot hills. Camped for noon on first branch of the Little Horn river. There is a settlement here which consists of eight or ten cabins scattered on river and creek in vicinity.

Traveled ten miles in the afternoon over a nice grassy country and only a few small snow drifts. Camped on second branch of Little Horn river. Grass much more forward in this valley. Used dead branches from wild plum trees for wood. There are many wild plum thickets along the streams and in the coulees but they seem to be dying out and the bear break them down and many are destroyed by the prairie fires, as are also the cherry bushes which are very numerous. Plenty of box elder and a little ash timber on these two creeks and they have rocky bottoms and stock can drink from them and cross them almost anywhere without danger of miring. It is a fine stock region. Saw many white-tailed deer today and yesterday but did not kill any as we did not need the meat.

Our horses are getting played out especially Bessie, the pack mule. I must buy some fresh ones as soon as I get a chance.

MAY 4. Broke camp at 7:30. Grass was good at this camp and our horses had all that they could eat and rested up. Plenty of green grass about three inches high everywhere. Traveled four miles over rolling grassy hills to Little Horn river. Charming country. Stream about the size of Flint creek and heavily timbered with ash, box elder and cottonwood and more willows than usual. Stream swift flowing over gravely bed with low banks and clear water. Stock can get in and out any where and there is a beautiful low bench on west side of the creek about one mile wide and eight miles long. Lots of deer here. Went eight miles over a high grassy ridge with water in all the ravines to Grass Lodge creek which is also a clear stream with low banks and rocky bottom. Considerable ash and box elder with a wide belt of willows along the stream;

more than we have seen anywhere on the trip. The
valley is not so wide as that of the Little Horn but there
are beautiful low grassy hills on either side.

Crossed a small creek in about three miles and in
three more came to Rotten Grass creek, clear and with
low banks and rocky bottom. In two miles more we
crossed Soap creek and then camped for the night.
Finest grass all over a rather hilly country which has
all been burned off last fall clear to the Big Horn river.
A constant succession of plum thickets on this stream.
There are plum bushes in every sag and ravine and
they are just beginning to blossom. The air is filled
with their sweet fragrance. The timber along here is
box elder and large willows. Deer and antelope in
sight all the time and a great number of prairie chickens everywhere. 'Tis very pleasant to hear the larks,
flickers, black birds, and curlews all singing every
morning early. The frogs croak all the time day and
night. Traveled twenty-two miles this day. Elevation 4000 feet.

MAY 5. Started at 7:40 A. M. and crossed a high
grassy ridge to a little creek that empties into the Big
Horn river just below the ruins of old Fort C. F.
Smith.[112] Went down the creek to the fort. The
ruins of the fort are of red adobe. It was once quite
extensive and very well built. It stands on a high
bench about sixty feet above the Big Horn river and
about three hundred feet from it. What a shame for
the government to allow the hostile Sioux to burn it
down. Visited the cemetery which is on a high part
of the bench four hundred yards southwest. There is

---

[112] Fort C. F. Smith was built in 1866 on the Big Horn to protect the
Bozeman road. It was abandoned in 1868 after the Fetterman massacre.
For history see *Ibid.*, pp. 135-146. – ED.

a nice monument of white marble but the Indians have shot it in several places knocking off some of the corners but it is still in fair condition.   Most of the head boards have rotted down but most of the names are on the monument.   Just above this graveyard a little creek comes in from the south and right at the mouth of this creek on the river bank is where the Crows fired into my brother James's party on the night of May 12, 1863, killing two and wounding seven.

Elevation of [Fort] C. F. Smith 3700 feet.   Went down ten miles further to the mouth of Rotten Grass creek and camped.   A furious wind was blowing that raised clouds of sand from the bars on Big Horn.   We could hardly get our tent up.   It began to rain at dark. The grass along here is four inches high.   There is an abundance of fine hay land all along and fine grass on hills and benches.   Traveled twenty-three miles this day.

MAY 6.   Traveled down Big Horn river ten miles and then turned east to go over to Little Horn river distance about fifteen miles over some high bad land hills but generally well grassed but with considerable sage however.   Went and visited the place where Reno fortified himself on the hill at the time of the Custer massacre.

Picked up some mementoes of the fight and camped for the night on the Little Horn about two miles below or half way between Reno hill and where Custer and his men were killed.   Their monument is in sight on the point of the ridge where they fell.   The river is about fifty or sixty yards wide and about thirty-eight inches deep on an average and very swift.   Considerable timber in clumps but not much underbrush.   There is some very good ash and box elder and fine grass.

The green grass is six inches high. Long slopes and
ridges on west side of Little Horn between it and the
Big Horn river well grassed and somewhat broken
country on east side extending back to Rosebud mountains only tolerably grassed and with much short
stunted sage and short-cut bank coulees extending back
a short distance from the river. Cloud peak and most
of Big Horn mountains visible from this camp. Elevation 3200 feet. Traveled thirty miles this day.

MAY 7. In the morning we went up to the battle
field and walked all over it. Saw just where the men
and horses fell. The bodies were placed in shallow
graves and covered with loose earth. I made some
sketches of the battle and picked up some shells. Cut
some ash canes at the place where Custer tried to cross
the river and was driven back and from there we returned to camp and packed up, came back, and followed the route taken by them which was marked by
bones of horses and graves of men marked by a stake at
their head. The first stand was made by a few in a
little sag near the top of the ridge where were the bones
of several horses and the graves of several men. This
was about a quarter of a mile from the river and from
there they curved to the left along the crest of the ridge
for about five hundred yards further where Custer and
the last of his men fell. Keogh and his men were killed
in a sag on the north side of this ridge. Custer and
others at the west end of the ridge. Bones of men and
horses are scattered all along between. On the point
where Custer fell is built up a sort of pyramid of cord
wood with a ditch around it and inside filled with bones
of horses. I found two battered bullets and many
empty shells. This ridge is not steep and is covered
with short grass and low stunted sage and a person can

gallop a horse over nearly any part of it.   The ground
rises steep about thirty feet in a sort of bench and then
slopes back gradually to the fatal ridge.   There are
some small sags and ravines running back to it also.
The field is a ghastly sight.

Went down to Fort Custer and bought some provisions and had some of the horses shod and was ferried
over the Big Horn and camped on the west bank.
Elevation 3100 feet.   Traveled sixteen miles this day.

MAY 8.   Rained in the night and is raining and
snowing a little this morning with a high west wind
and very raw and cold.   The bluffs on both sides of the
river are white with snow.   We concluded to wait a
little for it to clear up.

Fort Keogh [113] is on a high point of bluff at the junction of Big and Little Horn rivers about one hundred
feet above the river and has a fine view of Big Horn
mountains and all the rest of the country and catches
all the wind that is going.   Little Horn river is gravelly
banks and bottom clear to its mouth and can be crossed
anywhere.

About noon it cleared up and we traveled down the
river eighteen miles to the Half Way ranch, which is
a beautiful place where the bluffs run down close to the
river and are more or less timbered with nice yellow
pine trees and castle rocks in places.   They run back
ten or twelve miles and are beautiful in form and have
lots of game in them.   The Big Horn river is heavily
timbered with good cottonwood and some ash.   The
bluffs on west side of the river are distant six or eight
miles from where they begin, which is a little above
Fort Custer and gradually narrow in until they reach

---

[113] Fort Keogh was built by General Nelson A. Miles in 1877 as the
principal fort in eastern Montana.   Bancroft, *Montana*, p. 719. – ED.

the river at the Half Way ranch.   They are quite high
and level on top (to the west) and are well timbered
and form a beautiful back ground to the view.   The
land is all good.   There is but little water but it can
be brought from the river.   This would be an ideal
cattle range but it is on the Crow Indian reservation
consequently out of the question.   Big Horn and Pryor
mountains visible from Half Way house.   Elevation
2990 feet.   Traveled eighteen miles this day.

SUNDAY, MAY 9, 1880.   Went down the river twelve
miles and camped at noon in the forks of the Yellowstone and Big Horn rivers for the purpose of looking
for my brother James's name, which with date he
carved in the sandstone cliff between the rivers, when
on the Yellowstone expedition 1863.[114]

Many portions of the cliffs (which are a soft sandstone which weathers badly) have fallen and my
brother's name I could not find.   I found some of his
comrades' names.   First cut in bold capitals is "D.
Underwood, May 6, 1863;" next, "W. Roach, May 6,
1863;" and then "G. Ives;" and between these last
some Indian has scratched a crude picture of an Indian
with a war bonnet on and a "coup" stick in his hand
seated on a horse.   This was the best drawn horse I
ever saw drawn by an Indian, and about twenty-five
yards to the west is faintly scratched "S. T. Laust" and
near it is "W. R." and close to this is "H," and the
water has run down and washed away the rest of the
name, but below is "May 6 18" and nearby to the right
is "G X Ives 1863."   This is very well executed and
to the right of it is "A S Blake May 6th 1863," and I
could find no more.   Went about two miles up the
Yellowstone river to Terry's landing where we ferried

114 See note 77. – ED.

to the north side and put our horses in stable. Tracks of six Sioux Indians (on foot) were found a few miles back of the landing and most of the inhabitants are out with their guns tracking them up. They tracked them into a thick bottom full of brush about three miles above town and set fire to it in the hope of burning them out but only a portion would burn and so they had to give them up. There is a telegraph and post office here. Elevation 2930 feet. Got $250.00 from a gambler, B. F. Williams. Gave him a check on First National bank of Helena for same. Only man in town with any money.

MAY 10, 1880. Hired John Roberts with rifle horse and pack horse for $50.00, to go with us the rest of the trip. The Crow Indians tell us that the country between here and Flat Willow is swarming with Sioux in parties from ten to ninety strong. The Crows keep pretty close tab on the Sioux but they lie so one can put no dependence in what they say. We will keep watch and with four fine Winchesters and two revolvers and plenty of ammunition we will be able to take care of ourselves. Left Terry's landing at 2 P. M. and traveled seventeen miles where we found a spring in a coulee and camped for the night. The first few miles was through rough broken bad lands with plenty of pine timber and some good grass and a little sage. Some clumps of cottonwood in coulees where the water stands in holes and is quite strong of alkali. There has been a large herd of buffalo across here lately and they have eaten the grass off close. Saw a herd of buffalo running across the hills east of our camp. Indians after them of course. Kept all our horses tied at the tent and stood guard. The Crows may be right and we may run into some Sioux yet. Killed an antelope this after-

noon and saw some black-tailed deer but did not get a
shot.   Traveled seventeen miles this day.

MAY 11, 1880.   Breakfasted at 5:30 A. M. and left
camp at 6:30 and traveled twenty-two miles and
camped at noon on Alkali creek about five miles from
the Musselshell river.   Water strong of alkali and
salty besides, although it runs a small stream with big
pools along its course.   Large bands of antelope and
hundreds of buffalo in every direction.   I killed one
at camp.   High rolling prairie country most of the way
after the first six miles from the Yellowstone to top of
divide, when there comes in some nice yellow pine
groves and the country breaks up into bad land bluffs
which extend to the Musselshell which is about six or
seven miles from the summit of divide.

After dinner we went five miles to Musselshell
where the country is black with buffalo and crossed
and camped one-half mile below at cabin of Jack
Allen and Bush, which is deserted.   In the cabin was a
fry pan, coffee-pot, gold pan, and a case knife and outside about a gallon of coal oil in a five gallon can.
Dead buffalo, dead wolves, and dead dogs are thick
around the cabin and the smell is not that of attar of
roses, and there is a lot of it such as it is.

The country, both bottom and hills, is all covered
with stunted sage and greasewood and but little grass.
There are petroleum indications all through here and
some day Montana will produce oil but it is worthless
now.   The myriads of buffalo have eaten out what little
grass there is so our poor horses will fare badly here.
The river water is cold and pleasant to drink and less
strong of alkali than the holes out of which we have
been drinking.   Saw pony tracks (17) not very fresh.
We think they are about ten days old, doubtless Sioux

Indians. Harry Wormsley and John Roberts stood guard tonight. Had to run out and shake our blankets to frighten the buffalo away from camp and to prevent their stampeding our horses.

MAY 12. Started at 7 A. M. over a rough country broken by ridges and coulees and all covered with stunted sage and greasewood and very little grass and ten thousand buffalo busily engaged in eating up what little there is. Took a northwest course for Flat Willow creek, leaving the Little Snowy range a little to the west of our course. The Snowies at this distance (probably sixty miles) look like a large hump of a ridge white with snow on top and black with timber below, and running northeast and southwest and to right is other lower black-looking mountains and buttes not snow covered. Buffalo by the thousands in every direction. Could have killed many as we traveled along but we did not need the meat so did not molest them. Tom Irvine killed an antelope and we took the tenderloin and the hams and went on and camped at noon at a hole of rain water in a little dry creek. Had to use buffalo chips to cook with, for the first time on the trip. While in this camp a band of antelope lay down on a point on one side of our horses and two old buffalo bulls on the other side are standing guard for us. Antelope and buffalo are very tame here. Will hardly run from us.

I will here mention that whenever there is water in all this country where I have been, the frogs sing both day and night and the birds also, at least the larks do. Heard a thrush or mountain mocking bird at our camp in Eighteen Mile coulee. It sang beautifully.

In the bad land ridges soon after leaving Musselshell are great numbers of apparently fossil fragments of fishes all of one kind, long and slim; picked up and kept a few specimens. In the afternoon we started at 3:25 P. M. Scant sage and greasewood soon played out and the hills and vales have here a rounded grassy appearance but it is mostly short curly buffalo grass and extends from here to Flat Willow creek some twenty miles and just before we halted for noon the bad land nature changed to gravelly rounded hills and ridges which extend to Flat Willow which is bounded on the south side by high sandstone cliffs. When we passed there were pools of rain water in many dry ravines and flats remaining from the big storm of April 23 and 24. Although this country has a well grassed appearance, it is very thin in places and is about all buffalo grass, short and curly. Feed is very poor since leaving the Yellowstone so we kept on traveling until we reached Flat Willow, although it took us until 8:30 P. M. When we reached Flat Willow we found the grass better than anywhere since we left the Big Horn but it is not as good even now as we found it on the Little Horn river and its tributaries and it is not so good a looking country for stock down here but comes next to it.

There are a few plum thickets and choke cherries and plenty of box elder, but no ash, and but little cottonwood or under brush. Deep rich soil. "Pike" Landusky and Jo Hamilton planted corn, potatoes, and turnips and they all grew. There is no doubt but that tomatoes, squash, pumpkins and such can be grown successfully here.

There are some yellow pines and cedar on the bluffs but not much and it is about eighteen miles up to the spur of the Snowies on the south side of the creek to good pine poles and logs. Flat Willow is about thirty to thirty-five feet wide with generally steep cut banks (muddy) but mostly gravel bottom. Water very muddy, like the Rosebud, and from three to four feet deep. Hard limestone water. Blue joint grass in the bottom but not usually thick enough for hay.

Landusky and Hamilton have three log cabins of one room each, dirt roof and dirt floor. They have a picket corral of box elder logs about seven or eight feet high and sixty feet square where they corral their horses every night and put a boy, Harry Morgan, out to watch them day times. The Sioux Indians raid this country regularly.

They tell us that the snow did not get over six inches deep at any time last winter and did not lay on the ground long at any time. Traveled forty-three miles this day.

MAY 13, 1880. Laid over all day and let our tired horses rest, as the grass is good and we can put them in the corral nights and need not stand guard. We take our meals with Landusky. John Healy is stopping with him and they are trapping beaver. They caught two she ones while we were there, one had four kittens and the other two. They have them in a box. I do not believe they will live and have begged them to put the poor things back into the creek. They have a garden and Andy, the negro who had his feet and hands so badly frozen some years ago at Carroll, is cooking for them. Harry Morgan (son of John Morgan and about fifteen years old) is horse-guard day times and the horses are all put in the corral at night. Plenty of good hay land around here and picturesque cliffs coming on the south side.

MAY 14, 1880. Rained quite a shower in the night and is very cloudy and cold, with a high wind blowing and looks rather stormy. After waiting until 9 A. M. for it to clear up, we packed up and lit out and when we were about five miles on our way, it began to rain. We kept on for about three miles until we found a place where we could get tent poles and dry wood to kindle the fire and then we camped. The rain soon turned to slushy snow and rain and was decidedly disagreeable. We finally got the tent up and cooked our dinner. In the afternoon it cleared but left it muddy. Tom Irvine and Hank Wormwood walked out to the bench about a mile and killed an antelope and brought in the tenderloins and hams and then three big elk walked out of the brush on to a little ridge and "sassed" us plenty, but we had meat and so would not kill them. Grass very good and creek gravelly bottomed and easily crossed. Traveled ten miles this day.

MAY 15. Traveled about eighteen miles up Flat Willow creek to Brown's trading post. This is where Bill Hamilton wintered and said it was such a fine place for cattle. Brown tells me that the snow was never more than ten inches deep at any time all winter and that it did not lay on the ground long at any time. There is good grass in the bottoms and on the rolling hills with beautiful groves of yellow pine but so far no fir or lodge pole pine. Creek still muddy but not so thick as below.

Passed about forty lodges of Piegan and North Blackfoot Indians a few miles from Brown's. Elevation at Brown's 4000 feet. Kept on for about ten miles over a charming rolling grass country with water in all the ravines and small creeks. There are magnificent groves of tall straight yellow pine trees. Snow must fall very deep along here because there are snow drifts in many of the sags and bends of ravines. The world

FIRST ATTEMPT AT ROPING
From an old photograph among the Granville Stuart papers

INDIANS STALKING BUFFALO
From an old drawing in the Granville Stuart papers
The Indians would cover themselves with coyote skins and approach
the herd without arousing alarm. They could then shoot as many as
they chose with bow and arrow and thus save powder and shot

could not beat this for a summer range and it is very very beautiful. Saw many elk and black-tailed deer and bands of antelope. Since leaving Flat Willow, all the little creeks are clear and much colder than any water we have had on this trip.

The Little Snowie mountains loom up to the southwest quite grandly. They have a large quantity of snow on them and the tops of them seem to be above timber line. To the north are the Judith mountains but they are not nearly so high or so well timbered as the Little Snowies and have only a few snow drifts on the south side. To the right of them a short distance, standing at the beginning of the plain, on rather rolling ridges of little height rises the "Black butte" which is a beautiful curved top cone. It is very high and very steep and can be seen a long distance and I presume is a favorite roosting place for Sioux horse-stealing parties.

Chamberlain's place is on McDonald creek. The ranch was visited about ten days ago by a party of ten Sioux Indians who stole all of Chamberlain's horses and a lot of ponies from some Red river half-breeds who were camped here. Strange we have not run into some of these war parties but so far we have played in luck and still have our horses and our scalps. Chamberlain says the snow was about twelve inches deep in January but it did not lay long and then all went off and but little more fell and that did not lay. Traveled three miles down the creek below Chamberlain's and camped for noon. Grass nice and green and about four inches high. There are large patches of choke cherries on the creek and quantities of bull berries and red hawthorn bushes.

Once in a while there is a very large old cottonwood

tree but no young growth of cottonwood at all. Went on down the creek about nine miles and camped for the night. Killed an elk and saw many more. Plenty of antelope, we see bands of them on all the ridges. There are lots of sage and prairie chickens all over the country but no ducks or geese. Shot the heads off of two prairie chickens with my Winchester and we had fried chicken for supper. The new grass is six inches high at our night camp. The box elder trees are getting quite green. Willows not so much so. There is a fine hay bottom about nine miles below Chamberlain's on the north side of the creek. It is about two miles long and from one-fourth to one-third miles wide.

Found Sioux tracks where a party of about six crossed the creek on foot. They are doubtless looking for horses and it won't be their fault if they travel far on foot. We will take no chances with our horses. There is timber on the bluffs on both sides of the creek sufficient for present use. Not very good but will do for building and for fence posts. No poles nearer than twenty miles or so.

The valley of McDonald creek is not wide only from one-half to three-fourths of a mile wide with the stream meandering from side to side. Bluffs not very high. Sometimes on the north side breaking down to sloping benches. There is good gramma and buffalo grass on the bottoms and benches, also some stunted sage among it along here and some greasewood, while up between Brown's & Chamberlain's there is a big growth of grass, some regular bunch grass and no sage. Up there on the foot-hills indications are that there is too much snow for cattle to stay all winter.

Camped in narrow bend of creek with good brush shelter and after supper we moved about a mile further down the creek and made our beds in the dense willow brush.   Tied all of our horses up short to avoid standing guard.   Our course was northeast a few miles and we crossed the ridge between McDonald and Ford creeks and from the top of it had a good look over the country.   Saw two considerable lakes one on each side of Ford creek.   Water in all these ravines and coulees but is probably not permanent.   Good grass in broken good shelter ground until we got on Ford creek side when it became rather short and thin and mixed with stunted sage.   Do not like the country north and east of McDonald creek.   Too much sage.

Traveled up Ford creek about twelve miles when the sage played out on the north side and it looks smooth and grassy north to Black butte and west to Judith mountains probably twenty or twenty-five miles but so far (noon) the grass is short being mostly buffalo grass. After dinner we kept on up Ford creek five miles, killed a black-tailed deer out of a band of six.   Took the meat and then crossed over through a pine forest of pretty fair timber and some good holes too, onto a branch of McDonald creek near the foot of divide between McDonald creek and Judith basin.   Good grass at camp.   Some splendid bunch grass on the benches between the creeks and along several little creeks and in the sage.

MAY 19.   Started out at 7:45 A. M. and traveled six or seven miles up the head branches of McDonald creek to the top of the divide between it and Judith basin.   Elevation of summit 4500 feet.   During this morning's travel we passed through the most beautiful timber thinly scattered along the hillsides and ravines. Mostly straight yellow pines but some fine fir trees also and plenty of both fit for saw logs.   No white pine for poles but many groves of quaking aspens along here. Saw some on the creek down near Chamberlain's and this is the only locality I have seen any at all since I struck the Yellowstone this side of Bozeman. Some yellow pines all along here and finest bunch and other grass all along. Went to twelve miles beyond the divide into the Judith basin and camped for noon between Juneau's fort and Bowles and Reeds place. Juneau has a little log stockade fort about 100x150 feet with two bastions at opposite corners, but the logs are so small that a bullet from any heavily charged gun such as a Sharps or Needle gun, would go right through them. It is neatly fixed up on the inside and the houses of the Red river half-breeds are in marked contrast to the posts of the white men through here. There is quite a settlement of Red river half-breeds here who are plowing and planting a crop. A war party of Sioux Indians came through here three nights ago and stole thirty head of their horses. If we had not been delayed by the storm we would have probably met them over near Black butte and would, in that case have had some fun.

From the top of the divide the view is grand. To the south loom up the Little Snowies, white to the foot. To the west rise the Belt mountains with some snowy peaks but not nearly so much snow as on the Little Snowies. To the northwest is the huge steep castillated-like mass of the Highwoods and to the north and near by are the Big Moccasin mountains, not very high or with much snow. To the northeast are the Judith mountains, rough but not very lofty and in the center of this grand panorama of mountains and at our feet lies the famous Judith basin. Now with the billowy hills covered with green grass it resembles an enormous lake. It is about sixty miles long and fifty wide. It has magnificent bunch grass but is too open and exposed for a cattle range and the snow too deep. The soil of the basin is very deep and fertile and it would be a splendid farming country if there was a market. Big Spring creek takes its rise in one big spring up at the base of the Little Snowies and here at Juneau's it is twenty-five yards wide and two feet deep and very rapid. A beautiful stream of clear cold water. There is no timber and but little brush in the basin here. The basin was all burned off last fall and the green grass is up so as to make good feed for our horses but it is three weeks behind the grass on the Big Horn. After dinner we took the old Carroll road and went up the valley across a high bench that runs down from the Little Snowies and after traveling nine miles camped on Beaver creek and used the remains of a squatter's abandoned shack for wood.

With the single exception of Cottonwood creek which we crossed two miles before we camped, there is not so much as a willow twig big enough to burn from Reed's ford clear over to Judith gap and on to Hopley hole a distance of sixty miles. There is water in every coulee at this time of the year and little creeks of permanent water every few miles. There is a cold northeast wind and storming on the mountains. This is a cold bleak region and there are snow drifts still under banks and in ravines.

MAY 20, 1880. Left camp at 8 A. M. cold raw southeast wind, traveled twenty-five miles and camped at 2:30 P. M. at a little shack on a small creek about five miles north of the divide. Not a twig of wood on the road or at camp so had to take some of the roof poles to cook with. Here is the turning off place to the Yogo mines. Mr. Barrows came along and reports six steamboats already arrived at Fort Benton and more expected daily. The Yogo mines are not paying anything yet and I fear they are a failure. Snow drifts quite plentiful as we near Judith gap and the wind is very cold. Elevation here 4650 feet.

MAY 21, 1880. It rained all night. Got up late and saw an antelope within gunshot from camp and a buffalo bull still closer behind the tent. Tom Irvine took a shot at the buffalo but did not give him a mortal wound, followed him a quarter of a mile and killed him. Took the tongue and tenderloin. The weather cleared and we struck camp about 9:30 A. M. and traveled twenty miles. Camped for noon at Hopley hole. No wood on the road and the grass thin and poor except at Severen's sheep ranch where there is a large bottom of hay land. This side so far is not nearly so good a country as east of the Snowies on McDonald and Flat Willow (for grass timber or shelter). Hopley hole is a deep narrow valley sunk down one hundred fifty feet below the level of the table land or high bench which extends from the base of the mountains down to the Musselshell river.

Our camp was in a ravine on the west side of Hopley's hole which has many huge snow drifts in it. Used buffalo chips for cooking our dinner. Let our horses feed until 4 o'clock and then went on to Daisy Dean creek which we reached at 7:45 P. M. Could find neither wood nor grass sooner. We had nothing but small willows for fuel and it was very cold. Daisy Dean creek is narrow, deep, and very muddy, and ice one-half inch thick froze in our water bucket. Traveled thirty-seven miles this day.

MAY 22, 1880. Packed up and left camp at 8 A. M. and traveled four miles to Martinsdale at forks of the Musselshell. This town consists of four or five houses scattered over a mile or so of ground. There are thirty soldiers stationed here, and it is a good safe place for them as there are some settlers below to keep the Indians off them and the big spring roundup of cattle is now commencing and there are fifty men camped here who will work down the river fifty or sixty miles, so the soldiers are reasonably well protected. Here I parted with my companions Thos. H. Irvine, Hank Wormwood, and John Roberts who return from here to the Yellowstone. Paid Irvine $125, Roberts $50, and Wormwood $40. They are good men and true.

My horses are about exhausted and I have them with W. D. Flowers until I come back this way and I will go on to Helena by stage. High wind and very cold. Traveled four miles this day.

SUNDAY, May 23, 1880. Had to spend the day here and so stopped at R. H. Glendenning hotel, store, and post office. Stage does not go until tomorrow. Snowed about one inch early this morning and is very cold with flying snow squalls on the mountains. It looks as though there would be no spring this year. North and South forks of the Musselshell are both very high. No grass here, eaten into the ground. I wonder that the cattle here did not all die last winter. There are big snow drifts in all the sags and ravines and under banks. No timber but a few little cottonwoods along the stream and some yellow pine and fir twelve miles off on steep mountains. All the streams along here are muddy. I certainly would not select this for a cattle range but I presume there are five thousand cattle in here now.

Four of the six houses that I mentioned are saloons

and the brand of whiskey must be bad for the inhabitants "whooped her up" all night and I cannot say that I passed a quiet, peaceful Sabbath.

MAY 24. Started at 8:30 on the stage (big old open wagon) for Helena. Ten miles above the North fork is a very picturesque cañon with good yellow pine timber. A man by the name of Hall is building a sawmill here, so goodby to the lovely pines. They will soon all be sawed into lumber. Took dinner at Copperapolis, only three cabins and but one of them inhabited. Arrived at White Sulphur Springs at 7 P. M. A pretty valley here and rather agreeable broken grass country with groves of yellow pine and firs on the high hills on the way here. Lots of big snow drifts that are hard frozen and bear up the stage and horses, to my surprise. Elevation at Copperapolis 5600 feet; at White Sulphur Springs 5000 feet. There are some hot springs here strong of sulphur and said to be a sure cure for rheumatism. Have no thermometer so cannot get temperature. Had a bath in the water. Very agreeable only for the sulphur smell.

MAY 25, 1880. The coach left for Helena at 4 A. M. so we breakfasted at 3:30 A. M. Good hot coffee and venison steak and flapjacks. Raining cold and disagreeable and I was the only passenger. Snowed very hard while crossing over the mountains into the head of Confederate gulch and then it turned to rain as we descended the mountain. Had dinner at Diamond City, now a mere wreck of a once prosperous placer mining camp.

MAY 26-27-28, 1880. Remained at home answering letters and meeting my co-partners in the cattle venture and giving in my report and then went over to Deer Lodge to arrange to start the cattle toward the range.

I have decided to locate on Little Big Horn if I can lease grazing land from the Crow Indians, if not then, I will locate somewhere in Flat Willow country. Telegraphed to B. F. White at the terminus of the Utah Northern R. R. to know if the Crow Indian delegation and agent had arrived on their way home from Washington and received answer that they had just arrived. I determined to intercept them at Bozeman and interview them as to getting a lease to graze our cattle on the Big and Little Horn rivers.

JUNE 2, 1880. Met Agent Keller, two interpreters (Tom Stuart and A. M. Iurvey) and six Crow chiefs (Two Belly, Plenty Cow, Long Elk, Old Crow, Medicine Crow) at Gallatin and went with them to Bozeman where I was agreeably surprised to meet Colonel Pickett and Capt. Henry Belknap. The former hunts all the time and the latter has located a cattle range on Stinking river (fork of Big Horn). Agent Keller desired me to go to the agency before trying the Indians.

JUNE 6, 1880. Interviewed Agent Keller this morning. He is afraid to mention the matter to the Indians lest they should refuse to ratify the cession of the upper end of their reservation so I started on my return home at 10 A. M. in the usual rain storm. Remained in Helena until June 16 when I started for Sun River arriving there on the seventeenth. Remained in Sun River one day and sent one wagon and seven men to join Swett and go with him to Beaverhead to receive a small herd of cattle there. I took four men with me and started for Flat Willow creek via Fort Benton with a light wagon, two horses and six saddle horses. Country much cut up by ravines, and remnants of two ancient high benches are visible on foot of the mountains. Traveled sixteen miles this day.

MONDAY, June 20. Struck camp at 6 A. M. and traveled fifteen miles to Alkali creek at the north foot of Square butte, which should be called Table butte, for it is not square at all but is level on top and very high. Square (or Table) butte is evidently the point from which a great outpouring of lava or basalt took place and spreads over the adjacent country. It rises about two thousand feet above the plain at its foot and is very steep. Running down its sides in every direction are tremendous basaltic or try-dykes which stand up in narrow precipitious, jagged comb like ridges and about half way up it is surrounded by a belt of jagged irregular pinacles of basalt or trychyte while its summit, a plain about one-half to one and one-half miles long, is a table of series columnor basalt, which is verticle in most places from twenty-five to fifty feet. Under a cliff facing Arrow creek is quite a patch of seemingly good fir timber. This fork of Arrow creek is only in pools full of cattails and is strongly alkaline. Between Shonkin and Arrow creeks is a number of small lakes that seem permanent. Fine grazing country all over here. There is quite a number of cattle in here now and Henry McDonald has a band of two thousand sheep on Arrow creek. The Indians are also bad here and are continually stealing these people's horses. From Alkali creek we went ten miles down the fork to Arrow creek which is deeply sunken down in Bad Land bluffs. Good grass here in abundance. Ray Davenport and Kingsbury have about seventy-five head of thoroughbred short-horned cattle here. Met Mark Ainslie's bull team of fifteen wagons hauling Brown's and Allis' steam sawmill to Musselshell.

JUNE 22. We started at 6 A. M. but it took us an hour and a half to climb the fearful bad land hill on the

east side of Arrow creek.   Once on top we found ourselves on a vast plain.   To our right loomed up the
Square butte and Highwoods.   Due south is Judith
gap and just to the left of it is the long snow capped
ridge of the Little Snowies.   Away to the northeast
rises the blue and beautiful forms of the Bear Paw
mountains which are across the Missouri river.   Found
water in all the ravines between Arrow creek and Wolf
creek a distance of twelve miles.

We camped for noon on Wolf creek and caught a
few small fish.   After dinner we packed up and traveled fifteen miles to the forks of Sage creek which runs
but little water and looks as though it too went dry in
August.   Grass fine all over this country, but no wood,
not even willows and no shelter for cattle.   Saw quite
a herd of cattle (Power and Co.'s) on a small creek
before reaching Sage creek.   Sage creek is so named
because there is not so much as one sage bush on it.

We overtook and camped with some pilgrims who
are going to the Musselshell.   There was a small band
of antelope off on a ridge and I took my Winchester
and started after them.   One of the pilgrims went with
me.   He told me that he was a mighty hunter back in
Illinois.   I let him have the first try at the antelope but
he missed and they ran off.   I started back to camp
and he to follow the antelope.   My hunter friend did
not come in and when it begun to be dark his companions got uneasy about him.   Went out to the top of the
ridge and fired their guns several times and shouted.
No response.   Our party went to bed but the other side
of camp was restless and moving about and shouting
most of the night.   In the morning two of their party
were missing: the antelope hunter and another that
had gone to look for him.   None of these young fellows

have ever been out of town before, know nothing of this country and haven't the slightest idea of direction and are completely lost as soon as they are off the road. I told them to remain where they were and we would endeavor to locate their companions. Started my men out after the missing men. Found one sitting on a knoll about two miles from camp. The other we found eighteen miles from camp near the junction of Ross fork and the Judith river, completely lost and without presence of mind enough to look to see that the sun rose in the east.

The Judith is high, swift, and quite muddy owing to the placer mines at Yogo being on one of the branches. This whole basin is fine grass country but poor shelter for stock. There is water in all the coulees at this time of year. This whole basin is underlaid by regular bad land strata of dark colored clay and shale in nearly horizontal layers but its bad land character only shows when cut by the streams. There are antelope in sight almost all the time but only four or five in a band and they are wild. Camped for the night on Cottonwood creek about three miles below the Carroll road.

JUNE 24, 1880. Started at 6:10 A. M. and went on past Bowle's fort and Juneau's fort and camped for noon at the foot of Judith mountains about four miles east of Juneau's fort. In the afternoon went about three miles beyond the divide and camped for the night on a branch of McDonald creek.

JUNE 25. Started for Chamberlain's place on Mc-Donald creek. On our way down overtook about fifty carts of Red river half-breeds who have just moved over here from Judith basin and are going to Flat Willow and beyond to hunt buffalo. They have carts with two very large wheels in which the families ride.

They made a peculiar "screaky" noise that can be heard for miles.

JUNE 26, 1880.   Maillette, Grant, Cameron, and I traveled down McDonald creek about fifteen miles looking for hay land but did not find anything to suit. Saw two doe elk and four fawns.   Grant Gorden wanted to kill one but I begged him not to do it as the does would be poor and the fawns too young to eat, so he finally put his rifle back in the sling and let the pretty wild things live.   We crossed over to Good Luck creek about three miles and here found fifteen cow elk with some calves.   The boys would run them and Cameron killed a fawn, which we took to camp. Did not find any good hay land on Good Luck creek and the water tasted like slough water because of so many old beaver dams.   It is a pretty smooth grassy country here but there is no timber excepting box elder and willow.   Rode forty miles today over a beautiful grassy country but with little wood and still less hay land.   Returned to Chamberlain's.   About forty more carts and half-breed families arrived.   Came from toward Black butte.   Joined these already here which now make quite a village of lodges and carts.

SUNDAY, June 28, 1880.   This morning I went down to the half-breed village to inquire of them about hay land streams and the country in general.   Sevire Hamlin, quite an intelligent one, tells me that he knows just the sort of place I am looking for.   Hired him to take me to the place.   At 9:30 Maillet, James Heilman, and I, with Sevire Hamlin as guide, started out for Judith mountains.   Traveled slowly and camped at sundown at a spring in a patch of willows where we were sheltered from a disagreeable wind.   In the morning we traveled about three miles to a creek on which were some small groves of cottonwood. Stream of clear cold water and here about two miles from the mountains we found a magnificent body of hay land with cold springs all through it. This is the very place we have been hunting for. The whole country clear to the Yellowstone is good grass country with some sage and all of this country for a hundred miles in every direction is well grassed, well watered, and good shelter. There is an abundance of yellow pine and poles for all fencing and building purposes at the foot of Judith mountains. This is an ideal cattle range. They tell me it does not snow deep and it cannot lay on the ground because there is too much wind. Returned to Chamberlain's, seeing some splendid range on the way.

JUNE 30, 1880. Spent the day looking around and tried to buy Chamberlain out but he asked too much. I offered him $250 for four tons of wild hay and his two small cabins but he wanted $500, too much. Instructed the three men Cameron, Heilman, and Grant to lay foundation logs for seven claims. Two claims above Chamberlain, two up the creek near his hay land and three in three bottoms below. None of this land is surveyed and the only way to hold it is by occupying it. This meadow land I intend for a winter range station. Maillet and I then started for the big hay meadow on the head of Ford creek to lay three foundations there for claims. I intend to make this the home ranch for the outfit.

Life on the Cattle Range

As soon as I reached Helena I made our arrangements to start the various herds of cattle to the range and then hurried back to attend to locating the home ranch.

I selected a spot on Ford's creek near some nice cold springs, about three miles from the foot of Judith mountains, and began the construction of a log stable that would accommodate ten horses, a cabin for cowboys, and a blacksmith shop. These buildings formed two sides of a large corral.

We also built two log houses one for Reece Anderson's family and one for my own use. These houses formed two sides of an open square and as Indians were likely to be troublesome in that section of the country, the two houses were connected with a bastion like those used at the early trading posts. I located one thousand acres of hay land and later acquired title to about four hundred acres using soldiers' scrip principally. This land was fenced with barbed wire fences as soon as we could get the material.

In July, 1880, Fort Maginnis was established by Capt. Dangerfield Park. The location for the cantonment was on the upper end of the hay meadow that I had selected for my home ranch. In spite of my best efforts at persuasion they included more than half the meadow in their reservation. It was annoying to loose the hay land but the fort was a convenience as it furnished telegraphic communications, post office and a convenient place to purchase supplies.

By the first of October we had our buildings completed, some range cabins built, and five thousand head of cattle on the range and sixty head of horses.

Two companies of the Third Infantry were at Fort Maginnis. Mrs. Fitzgerald and three children, family of the post tailor was the first family to arrive. About the middle of October Mrs. John T. Athey, wife of the post trader, arrived. The first notice I had of her being there was when a sergeant appeared at my door with an empty bed tick under his arm and told me that Mr. Athey had sent him down to have it filled with "Montana feathers." We had cut some fragrant sweet grass in the meadow during the summer so I sent the tick down to the stack and had it filled with the sweet-smelling hay. Mrs. Athey told me afterward that it was the most luxurious bed she had ever rested on.

In the early spring a baby girl was born to the wife of Frederick France at the fort. This was the first white child born in this section of the country and we could no longer consider ourselves beyond the borders of civilization.

In November, 1880, all bids for furnishing beef to Fort Maginnis were rejected by the commander as being too high. They then purchased twenty-five head of beef steers on the Shonkin and sent a detachment of soldiers to drive them to the fort. The soldiers were entirely unfamiliar with the country and knew nothing about driving range cattle so had trouble with them from the start and by the time they reached the crossing of the Judith river, they had lost about one-half of the bunch, and here they encountered a storm. The cattle stampeded and the soldiers became lost and bewildered but finally struck a trapper who kindly piloted them to the fort.

After this mishap the commander appealed to us and I finally agreed to furnish them beef that is I sold them four fat old steers delivered at Fort Maginnis for $45.00 per head, and they butchered them themselves.

The following year all bids were again refused, although they were lower than the ranchers were receiving at the mining camp of Maiden nearby. None of the cattle outfits sent in bids to furnish beef to the fort because they were all new on the range and busy getting located and could not keep extra men to attend to small orders.

This time the commander purchased a few head of beef steers on Flat Willow about twenty miles from the fort and again sent a detachment of soldiers to drive them to the fort. An accidental discharge of a shotgun stampeded the cattle and they scattered and could not be found. For weeks detachments of soldiers rode over the range chasing and disturbing our cattle greatly to our annoyance and detriment. These troopers were mostly of foreign extraction and from the East. They knew absolutely nothing about range stock and could not read a brand ten paces from an animal and were as incapable of taking care of themselves when out of sight of the post as three-year-old children.

We protested to the commander against allowing the soldiers to ride the range and chase and scatter our cattle but I failed to make him see how the soldiers riding about among wild range cattle and running the fat off them, could injure us or how it could be that we did not like it. I finally sent some cowboys out; rounded up the lost cattle and delivered them to the fort at our expense. I then invited the commander to dinner at the ranch and in an after dinner chat took occasion to explain to him the natural antipathy that a cowboy had for a soldier and that if they persisted in disturbing our cattle it would be at their own risk. We had no further trouble from that source for some time but it fell to my lot to furnish them beef. This time we butchered them at the ranch and the soldiers came and got the carcasses.

Our next trouble came in shape of a roving band of Cree Indians from Canada. The range riders notified me that they were killing the cattle. Taking two cowboys with me, I started for their village. There were about fifty men, women, and children in the party headed by a white man who claimed to be a Catholic priest. They had no provisions and were depending solely on the game that they could kill for sustenance.

I called for their chief and an old Indian came out to meet me. Pointing to a frozen beef hide thrown across a pole I asked for an explanation. The chief said his people were starving and game was scarce, that my cattle being on the range made the buffalo go away; that the priest told him that he had a right to kill the white man's cattle when his people were hungry. I asked him if he did not know that his hunting grounds were in Canada and not south of the Missouri river? He acknowledged that he was not in his own country but said that they could find nothing to eat there either and that the priest told him that it was right to kill our cattle when their children were hungry. I called for the priest and after a time he reluctantly appeared. I asked him what right he had to come on our range and advise the killing of our cattle? His excuse was that the women and children were hungry. I discovered that they had killed three steers, one cow, and one yearling. I ordered the chief to round up their horse herd and then selected five ponies to reim-

burse me for the slaughtered cattle, then told the chief
to leave the range at once. Some of the young Indians
protested at my taking their ponies and became quite
ugly. I called for the priest [115] and in dealing with
him was rather more emphatic, promising to hang him
higher than Haman if he ever set foot on the range
again. He and the Indians lost no time in getting
north of the British line. Roving bands of Canadian
Indians continued to harass us all winter.

The winter of 1880-81 was one of unusual severity;
our cattle were new on the range and not feeling at
home drifted badly. We had to watch every pass and
were kept busy turning them back on the range when
they had gone too far. Quite a number of the horses
evaded us in spite of our vigilance and returned to their
old homes. We had range cabins and kept range
riders out all winter looking after the cattle.

On December 8 eighteen inches of snow fell and the
thermometer registered thirty-two degrees below zero.
The storm lasted four days and from that time on until
May 15 there was a series of storms with the thermometer from twenty-two to forty degrees below zero. The
snow lay deep and many of the buffalo died. On our
range the snow did not lay long on the ground. The
hillsides were bare most of the winter but the gullies
and coulees were drifted full. A snow storm set in on
the fourteenth of January and two feet of snow lay on
the ground. It turned cold and mercury fell to twenty-
eight degrees below. The range looked and felt like
the Arctic regions.

On the evening of the seventeenth, I noticed flat pan-
cake chinook clouds in the western sky. The wind
began to roar on the mountains and blew so hard that

---

[115] I afterwards learned that this man was not a priest at all.

it was almost impossible to stand against it. At midnight the thermometer was forty-eight degrees above, the snow had disappeared and the gulches and coulees filled with water to a depth that would swim a horse. On the other side of the range, in the Judith basin there were three feet of snow. The Chinook did not reach them and the snow lay on the ground until the first of April.

The first year on the range we had no neighbors and as we had watched the cattle closely but few had strayed from the range. We rounded up alone, beginning May 25. Our losses all told, this first year were thirteen per cent, five per cent from Indians, five per cent from predatory animals and three per cent from the storms. The small loss from the storms was because there were so few cattle on the range; that feed was unlimited; and the creeks, and brush, and tall rye grass furnished them dry beds and shelter equal to a good stable and our cattle were northern range stock.

The same summer an English company drove five thousand head of cattle from Texas and located their home ranch at the mouth of Otter creek in Custer county. The cattle did not reach Montana until late in the fall and they were thin and worn from the long drive. Practically the entire herd perished. The sheriff of Custer county could find but one hundred and thirty-five head in the spring to satisfy a judgment held by Charles Savage of Miles City for supplies. The cowboys with the outfit were never paid their wages.

At this time (1880-81) the management of our Indian affairs was about as bad as it could well be and it was idle for us to hope for relief from wrongs that would have made Henry Ward Beecher swear like a trooper.

Let me review this delectable system and how it worked. First the government sets apart for each tribe enough of the choicest land to make a state; larger in fact than many of the older states of the Union, upon which the white man in search of homes may not put his foot, or even allow his domestic animals to feed upon the grasses which there grow up and decay without benefit to anyone, but the Indian who makes no use of this vast domain is allowed to leave at his own sweet will, and to stay away as long as he pleases and this he does for the well-known purpose of stealing the white men's horses, eating his cattle, and robbing his cabin. Time has no value to an Indian and he has no business that will suffer from his absence or neglect. He conceals himself in the timber and brush on the mountains or along the streams, for weeks or months, if necessary, subsisting off cattle killed as his needs require. His ideal of a good living is not a lofty one, and he is willing to submit to severe privations for the chance of finally stealing a horse, for a clever horse thief ranks next to a chief in an Indian tribe.

At last he secures his prize and by the time the victim discovers his loss the thief is fifty, sixty, or seventy miles away, for all Indians are desperate riders, and their flight always up to the limit of the speed and endurance of the horses stolen, and in this country unless a considerable number of horses are taken it is extremely difficult to find and follow the trail, and the loser is confronted with the question of, which direction did they go? for we are surrounded by Indian reservations, which means thieves. If found and followed,

the trail, of course leads to some reservation and we are
strictly forbidden to enter upon the poor Indians' little
patch of ground (usually about one hundred by a two
hundred miles square) without first obtaining the consent of a resident autocrat known as an "Indian agent"
who is the joint product of the "Indian ring" and some
village in the eastern states, where a careful study of
Cooper's novels and the equally truthful and rose-
colored reports of former Indian agents have convinced
the resident population that the western Indian is a
Christian gentleman of aesthetic tastes, with a child-
like and bland smile, and that the western pioneer is a
border ruffian and a villain, whose chief aim and object is to steal the purse, good looks, and clean shirts of
the noble red man, while he is attending church. First
the reservation, next the "agent," who is selected with
especial regard to his utter and absolute ignorance of
the Indian language, mode of life, habits, character,
and best methods of influencing and controlling the
nation's wards. Then come the united efforts of the
government and the agent to civilize and enlighten the
Indian, by so far as possible, isolating and cutting him
off from connection with civilization, as found and em-
bodied in all well-ordered communities of white men,
by wrapping his robe of savagery and barbarism more
closely about his filthy form, by concentrating him on
reservations far from the only known civilizing
agencies, contact and constant communication with the
superior race.

The system which herds the Indians together on re-
mote reservations, allows them to be armed and
mounted at all times and under the leadership of their
chiefs insures the propagation of all their old prejudices, lawlessness, and habits of thought and life, will

not civilize them in ten thousand years, for public opinion is as strong in an Indian village as in any white community. Public opinion among Indians is to assign to women the lot of a slave. She is considered a little better than his dog but not anywhere nearly so good as his horse. To her he kindly assigns everything in the shape of work connected with the Indian *menage*, while his duties consist in wearing grease paint and feathers. He also has a passion for going on the war path and stealing everything in sight within a radius of four hundred miles from his particular agency.

The annual appropriations of the government for several years has been ample to board everyone of the agency Indians, big and little at a first class hotel, yet somehow all of this money does not seem to fill a long felt want (or the Indians either) for he remains the same dirty poverty-stricken thief that he became when first placed on a reservation. It is well-known that everything brought from the east shrinks most awfully in this high dry altitude, yet this scientific fact would hardly account for the portly and robust appropriations becoming so thin and emaciated, that when they do finally reach the Indians they are like the darkies' fish, "all swump up." The Indian knows that he is being robbed and in turn becomes a thief. So long as these conditions prevail the cattlemen and the homesteaders remain the victims of the "system" and their only salvation lies in their ability to protect their property and look out for their scalps.

First we appealed to the Indian agents at the various agencies, notifying them of the presence of the Indians on the range and of the depredations they were committing and requested them to keep their Indians on their reservations. Some of our communications were answered and some were not. Major Lincoln, of the Fort Belknap reservation, kept the Gros Ventres at home demonstrating that it could be done and very few depredations were committed by that tribe. From some of the other agents we received fair promises but no action. Added to the trouble with our own Indians was that with the British Treaty Indians, the Crees, North Assiniboines, Bloods, North Piegans, Sarcees, and Sioux, all related to and speaking the language of our northern tribes.

Each autumn after their annual payments at Forts MacLeod and Walsh, these tribes swoop down upon us, their number carrying strength. They defy the white men, and the military pay no attention to them except to report to headquarters, and then inspect their forts and test their safety in case of an attack. Occasionally a squad of ten men and a lieutenant are sent out to "order the Indians to return at once" at which the chief would smile, grunt, ironically admire the brass buttons on the blue coats, and pay not the least bit of attention to the order. The Indians continued on their way robbing ranches, frightening women, stealing horses and subsisting on our cattle.

Between the months of November, 1880, and April, 1881, three thousand head of cattle were wantonly butchered by Indians in Choteau and Meagher counties; there was therefore in six months a destruction of $60,000.00 worth of property by the malice of Indians.

Losses of this magnitude from one source alone could no longer be borne by the stockmen. We had also discovered that someone was furnishing whiskey to the Indians which partially explained the inordinate desire of the Indians to spend so much of his leisure on the range. An Indian would part with his last pony, dog, child or wife, or barter his blanket or last pound of flour, steal or commit murder in order to get whiskey. A sober plain Indian was bad enough but when crazed by the rot-gut whiskey peddled to him by the human ghouls that prowled around the border of the reservation, he became a raving savage maniac, a peril to everybody within his reach.

These whiskey peddling fiends were not allowed on the reservations and if caught they were severely punished but located at convenient places on the range masquerading as trappers or wood choppers they plied their nefarious trade in safety, as the Indians would never tell where they got their whiskey. These whiskey traders would visit an Indian village; sell or barter what whiskey they had and then clear out of that neighborhood as speedily as possible, leaving the Indians to consume the fire-water and then do whatever their savage instincts prompted them to do. A drunken orgy at one of these isolated villages, where crazed savages beat, abused and mutilated their women and children; cut, slashed, and shot each other, beggars description.

Horses were the most desirable property for trade so when the whiskey trader had all that the Indian had he simply "lit out" and stole more horses and traded them for more whiskey. These whiskey traders were well aware that most of the horses that they traded for were stolen property, for Indian ponies have no harness marks or shoes on them. They would drive them to places in the bad lands, where it was impossible to find them unless perchance one accidently stumbled on them, remove their shoes, if they had any, change the brands and hold them there until they could drive them east into Dakota or north across the British line and dispose of them.

Confronted with these enormous losses the young struggling stock-growing industry faced certain annihilation unless immediate steps should be taken to protect it. M. E. Milner, secretary of the Shonkin Stock Association, called a meeting of the stock men of Choteau and Meagher counties at Fort Benton on August 15, 1881, for the purpose of organizing a stock protective association. The meeting was well attended in spite of the fact that many of the stockmen were out on the roundup, I being one of that number. We sent letters, which were read at the meeting, promising our hearty co-operation in any measure that gave promise of protection to our property.

At this meeting the executive committee appointed one stock man residing at Fort Benton, to accompany Sheriff John J. Healey on all expeditions taken in behalf of the Stock Protective Association, who was to be paid by the association. A reward of $500 was offered by the association for the apprehension and conviction of any person or persons selling, bartering, or giving whiskey to Indians on the ranges of stockmen, members of that association. A reward of $100 was offered by the association for the apprehension and conviction of any persons detected in selling or giving intoxicating drinks to half-breeds upon the range. A reward of $500 was offered for the apprehension and conviction of any person or persons maliciously or carelessly setting out fires on the range. A standing advertisement to the above effect stating the rewards offered was ordered inserted in the Fort Benton papers.

It was further decided that the association hire men

at its own expense to ride range and look after Indians. Canadian Indians were to be intercepted at the border, ordered back across the line; if they went peaceably, well and good, but if they persisted in coming through the range, they did so at their peril, and the final issue would be raised then and there. Our own Indians were to be treated in the same manner. Stealing horses and stealing cattle would no longer be tolerated.

Hon. Martin Maginnis, our delegate in Congress, was called upon to address the meeting. Mr. Maginnis said he coincided with the views expressed by members and approved of the movement they had set on foot. While he deprecated any action that would lead to a war with the Indians, he could not but sympathize with the stockmen in the present case. If the government refused to extend its strong arm for the protection of the citizens of northern Montana, there was no recourse left them but to protect their own property and it was natural that they should do so.

The Major stated that in the past he had done all in his power to obtain redress of wrongs suffered by stockmen, but without any good result. While claims presented were generally allowed by the proper officer, Congress would not appropriate money to meet these demands, already amounting to several millions. He promised at the coming session of Congress to put forth his best efforts to secure relief for the stockmen and to see to it if possible that the British Indians did not commit further depredations on American soil. As soon as the Stockgrowers Protective Association was organized and their proposed action made public, a great hue and cry went up over a threatened Indian war that the stockmen were about to precipitate. The whiskey peddlers were loudest and most active in spreading the alarm. They proclaimed from the house tops that homesteaders were being driven from their homes and their property confiscated by the cattle men. Much was said about the attitude of Great Britain and that she would not stand for any interference with her Treaty Indians and that an international clash was inevitable. Strange as it may seem, our leading newspapers published all of these lurid alarms with large headlines and on front pages. A call for more troops for the frontier was sent in. General Terry, then commander of the division of the Northwest, stationed at Fort Snelling, said that he could spare no more troops. Everything possible was published and sent broadcast that would lead the general public to believe that the cattle men were encroaching on the Indians as well as small ranchers or "nestors" as they were called. At the same time these whiskey traders were not producing a single dollar and were doing more to degrade and debase the Indian and to endanger the lives and property of white settlers than all the cattlemen in Christendom ever could do.

The stockmen took no little pains to track up and find the source of these stories about homesteaders being driven from their ranches by cowpunchers. Invariably they were traced to the whiskey traders. One story in particular had a wide circulation and created something of a sensation.

Mrs. Annie Boyd came driving into Bozeman with six small children in the wagon box and a baby in her arms. She told the authorities that her husband had located a ranch on the Yellowstone and that while he was absent from home working, cowboys had come to the ranch and ordered her to leave the place. She was ill in bed, having a baby but ten days old so she could not go, but remained in terror for ten days when they again appeared at the ranch, caught up the team and hitched it to the wagon, then throwing in some provisions and loading in the children they ordered her to drive on and not to stop on that range again.

I was eating my breakfast in the Leland hotel in Chicago, when a benevolent old gentleman, knowing that I was from Montana, handed me the *Chicago Times* with the story copied from a Bozeman paper. I knew that there was no truth in it but determined to track it and see if it had a foundation. That afternoon I purchased my ticket to Bozeman instead of Helena.

I found Mrs. Boyd in Bozeman where she was being nicely cared for by sympathizing citizens and heard her very graphic but "fishy" story. My next move was to visit the Crow agency and there I learned that Mrs. Boyd's very hard working husband had taken refuge across the British line where he had fled to escape arrest for selling whiskey to the Crow Indians. He had located on the Crow reservation and the agent had ordered this family to leave and when they failed to go, he had sent the agency police to eject them. The Boyds were not on the cattle range and no stockman or cowboy had ever seen or spoken to them.

When Congress convened, Delegate Maginnis sent a letter to the Secretary of the Interior in which he called attention to the grievances of the stockmen of northern Montana and the steps they had taken to prevent further depredations by Indians on the range. Major Maginnis called the attention of the department to the fact that losses sustained by citizens of Montana, heretofore had never been paid by the government, so that they seemed to have no recourse but to defend their property by force if necessary. He sought to impress the fact that a few collisions between the stockmen and Indians might result in a bloody and expensive war and asked that prompt action be taken to prevent impending conflicts. He also made it clear that there never was any excuse for permitting British Indians to cross the line and commit depredations on our people. He made it quite clear to the department that unless the Indians were kept on their ample reservations that trouble was sure to ensue.

The Secretary addressed the following letter to the Commissioner of Indian affairs and there the matter rested so far as they were concerned, until this good hour.

Department of Interior,
Washington, September 15, 1881.

To the Commissioner of Indian Affairs:

Sir: I am in receipt of a letter from the Hon. Martin Maginnis, Delegate in Congress from Montana Territory enclosing a letter from Hon. Granville Stuart, of Helena, M. T., relative to the threatened disturbances between the settlers and Indians upon the Blackfeet Reservation in said Territory.

The treaty of October 17, 1855, with the Blackfeet and other tribes of Indians mentioned therein (article 3) allows certain lands therein noted to be used and considered as common hunting ground for ninety-nine (99) years. These lands have been penetrated by stock raisers who represent very heavy interests in the Territory, and it is complained on their part that these Indians are in the habit of committing depredations upon them by wantonly killing and destroying their stock.

Article 7 of the said treaty (vol. II, p. 958) allows citizens of the U. S. to live in and pass unmolested through the country.

Article 11 of said treaty provides that any property taken by the Indians, or injured or destroyed shall be paid for out of their annuities and article 12 provides that in case of violation of this treaty, their annuities may be withheld.

I have requested that you will communicate with the agent having control over the tribes of Indians above indicated upon the subject matter of the letter of Mr. Maginnis and its enclosure and instruct them in all cases where hunting permits are hereafter issued to Indians under their charge, a capable and efficient employee of the agency should accompany each party, to watch over the Indians and prevent any depredations on their part.

In the present temper of the settlers, slight provocation might precipitate a conflict between them and the Indians, the result of which would be deplorable and such difficulty should be avoided by every effort possible in the power of the Agents.

Very respectfully,

S. J. KIRKWOOD, Secretary.

Just as we expected all these documents were carefully pigeonholed in accordance with the best government usage and the stockmen left just where they were before and that was not to expect help from the government, but to work out their salvation in their own way.

We did not have to wait long before the opportunity to try our methods came to us. In August a band of Canadian Indians raided the Yellowstone, driving off twenty-five head of good American horses belonging to three ranchers, Brown, Harrison, and Murray. Immediately after the stockmen's meeting Sheriff Healey accompanied by his deputy and Mr. Harris started north to look for the horses, two of which they found on the Blackfeet reservation, right at the agency and directly under the eye of the agent. He also captured Bad Bull, a Blood Indian, belonging to the band of Bull-who-goes-'round and brought him back to Benton in irons. Bad Bull was an ugly customer and gave his captors no little trouble by resisting arrest and by his attempts to escape. He was held as hostage at Benton and word sent north to his friends and relatives that he would not be released until the stolen horses were recovered.

Failing to recover all the horses stolen, Mr. Harrison accompanied by the Piegan chief, White Calf, and seven warriors, continued the journey north to Fort McLeod with every assurance of finding them among the Bloods at the agency. When they reached the agency a search was instituted in a quiet way for the horses but none could be found. Thereupon Calf Shirt summoned the chief of the Bloods to conference with Mr. Harrison. He was told that all that was wanted was the stolen horses. The Blood chief went away and soon returned with a few head of horses, some of them Harrison's, all in a miserable condition. He reported that these were all that were in camp, but Harrison suspected, and the event proved it so, that the best horses had been sent for trade with the Kootenais and after buffalo. Thereupon application was made to Major James Crozier, commandant of Fort McLeod, for assistance. Major Crozier had been aware of a war party of thirty Indians having come back from across the line with white men's horses a few days before. He immediately sent out some mounted policemen and in a few hours they had brought in seven of the party – all that could be found, to the fort.

A jury of twelve citizens was impaneled and the trial held before Colonel McLeod. In less than two hours and a half, the seven Indians were found guilty. Sentence was suspended fearing that it might make the remainder of the party, for whom search was being made, get out of the country.

These forcible and summary measures had a good effect on the Indians; the first of which was the surrender of eighteen head of horses which had been stolen from time to time. All of these horses were turned over to Sheriff Healy who in turn restored them to their owners.

The first action taken by stockmen to protect their own property proved that the British government was as anxious to keep their Indians at home, as we were to have them and that if complaint was made to the authorities, that their methods of capturing and punishing the thieves and restoring stolen property was both expeditious and effective. The Indians were shown conclusively that they could no longer steal horses in the United States, drive them across the line and remain there with them in safety.

It was further proven that if the Indians were made to understand that they could no longer run about over the range, drink whiskey, kill cattle and steal horses, without paying the penalty then and there: that they would remain on their reservations and without the slightest danger of Indian war. An Indian's idea of war meant a big noise, a big bluff, lots of paint and feathers, and fancy riding; but when he finds that somebody is certain to be hurt and that there is neither bluff or noise he will calmly fold his blanket about him and retire to the friendly shelter of his reservation.

It was the custom of the British government to pay to their Treaty Indians the annual annuities in September, consequently some six thousand Indians assembled at Forts McLeod and Walsh at that time to receive their annuities, and as soon as they were paid would start for the cattle ranges where they would exchange their money for whiskey and there kill cattle and steal horses the rest of the winter. The Stock Protective Association was working without the law save that of self-protection from justly apprehended harm. For two years they took care of their Indian problems in this way and while it was not a complete success it was a step in the right direction. It put a check on cattle killing and horse stealing and partially rid the range of Indians. The Canadian mounted police at all times co-operated with us and rendered valuable assistance.

On the sixteenth day of September, 1881, a prairie fire started at Grass range and we sent a crew of men to put it out, when reports of fire on Crooked creek near Haystack butte were sent in and men hurried to that locality, then a disastrous fire near Black butte that threatened to destroy the horse ranch. Fires sprang up in all directions almost simultaneously and spread with alarming rapidity. The flames swept up McDonald creek at the rate of a mile a minute. Great columns of black smoke rolled up in every direction, filling the air with ashes and cinders. At night, lines of flame crept along the ridges, flinging a lurid glare against the sky line. For ten days every available man in the country, with wet gunny bags, fought the flames with desperation, some of them sinking in their tracks from exhaustion. In spite of almost superhuman efforts more then five hundred square miles of the finest grass land in eastern Montana lay a blackened waste.

We lost no fences or hay but the loss of much grass was a hardship as we had increased our herd by five thousand head of cattle and one hundred horses.

When we came to use our brand we found it blotched and was not plain so we changed it to "D-S" and the name of the company to Davis, Hauser, and Stuart. On the range an established cattle company was "an outfit" and everthing pertaining to it was known and called after the brand. From this time on, the ranch, cattle, horses, cowboys, and the owners were known as the "D-S" outfit.

We had had some ploughing done in the fall and in the early spring we planted forty acres of oats and a patch of potatoes. I set out an orchard of fifty fruit trees, apples and crab apples. The oats yielded one hundred bushels to the acre but the trees did not do well as there was a family of beaver in the creek just above where I planted the trees and they built a dam and flooded my orchard.

I did not want to kill the poor things and I did not want them to leave the ranch so I just tried to discourage them from building the dam at that particular place, by repeatedly tearing it out. It did no good for as often as I tore it out they rebuilt it in the self-same spot and I finally gave it up and let them have their dam and the trees all died with the exception of a few crab apple trees that stood out of the way of the flood. There were lots of wild strawberries in our meadows and gooseberries, choke cherries, and bull berries grow along the streams. We planted rhubarb, currants, and gooseberries, and all did well.

In the summer of 1881 James Fergus came to the range and located on Armell's creek. Kohrs and Bielenburg brought in three thousand cattle and turned them loose on Flat Willow. Power Brothers and Charles Belden brought two herds into the Judith basin, Robert Coburn and Henry Sieben had herds on Flat Willow. John Dovenspeck located on Elk creek. This spring the several outfits on the range "pooled," that is we all worked together as one outfit.

The first meeting was held at the D-S ranch on May 29, 1882, and the minutes of that meeting will give an idea of how we conducted the business. I acted as secretary of the meeting. Present, James Fergus, Andrew Fergus, N. J. Bielenburg, and N. J. Dovenspeck.

It was moved and carried that every stock owner have one vote for each rider furnished and employed by him on the range, and that all persons having one thousand or less cattle on the range be required to furnish one rider, or in lieu thereof pay the roundup fund $2.00 per head for branding and marking their calves, that being the price fixed for branding calves for those not attending. And that all owners having more than one thousand cattle on the range furnish one rider for each one thousand head or fraction of five hundred or over.

W. C. Burnett was nominated for Captain of the roundup and was unanimously elected, with pay at the rate of $2.50 per day from beginning to close of each roundup, to be paid out of roundup fund.

It was decided to send one man to the Musselshell to bring back any cattle from this range found there and to brand and mark all calves as found. It was decided that one man tally all calves branded and to see that there are turned out by their respective owners seven bull calves, to each one hundred heifer calves. N. J. Bielenburg was elected to attend to the same.

All mavericks were to be sold to the highest bidder at the corral, branded and marked and turned with the purchaser's herd. Only cattle owners on the range could purchase these calves. The money received from sale of mavericks shall be turned in to the roundup fund.

The spring roundup for 1882 is to begin on the north side of the range May 30. It was decided to begin the fall calf roundup Sept. 1 on the north side of the range, and the beef roundup to begin October 1 on the north side of the range.

It was decided to pay the day and night horse wranglers and the wood hauler out of the roundup funds. The men sent out to attend other roundups were also paid out of said fund.

On motion the meeting then adjourned.

GRANVILLE STUART, Sec.

In the fall we drove the beef to Fallon station on the Northern Pacific and shipped from there.

On this trip, while camped on the Porcupine, I found some peculiar round balls of very hard bad land clay about the size of a cocoanut, broke one open and inside was a mass of small fossil shells and the back bones of fish imprinted in the mud. I also noticed oil shale along the bad land cuts and extensive veins of coal along the Yellowstone. When the country settles these coal beds will be valuable.

In the fall I found that there were twelve children of school age within reach of the ranch so gave a room in the house for school purposes and organized a school district and had a six-months term of school. Miss Cecil Benda of St. Louis was our first teacher.

In the early range days the Texas system of everybody's placing his brand on every calf found unbranded on the range, without even trying to ascertain to whom the animal belonged, was in full vogue. From the first I took issue against this kind of business. It was only a step from "mavericking" to branding any calf without a brand and from that to changing brands. Cowboys permitted to brand promiscuously for a company soon found that they could as easily steal calves and brand for themselves. If we are to believe the stories that floated up from Texas to our range, a goodly number of big Texas outfits had their beginning without capital invested in anything save a branding iron. In the broad open country of the range a man's conscience is apt to become elastic. A strong stand against anything approaching cattle stealing must be taken if the industry was to thrive.

In spite of warnings and protests a goodly number of calves were being mavericked and many horses stolen. The thing of paramount importance to the stock growers was a strong association for the betterment of range conditions. In the fall of 1882 I was elected a member of the Thirteenth Legislative assembly and spent two months in Helena. The council was evenly divided politically and there was a contested seat, both parties claiming the member from Chouteau county. The council could not organize but after the usual amount of wrangling attending such an occasion I was selected as a compromise, and elected president of the council.

There were a number of cattlemen in the legislature and we made an attempt to pass some much needed laws to protect the rapidly growing range industry, and did succeed in getting a few measures through but some of the much needed ones failed to pass because of lack of information on the part of the members of the legislature and by the very hostile attitude of the newly appointed governor of the territory, John Schuyler Crosby.

Governor Crosby was from New York, a cultured gentleman, a delightful person to meet socially. He had spent most of his life on the staff of various generals of the army and in Europe but was entirely out of harmony with his surroundings in Montana and unfamiliar with the industries or the needs of the territory and he used his executive powers very freely, to veto legislative bills.

The centers of population were in the western part of the territory, and our chief industry had been mining, so it was not strange that but little attention had been given to the rapid changes taking place in the eastern part of the territory.

Failing to get the much needed laws passed to protect their property, the cattle men turned their attention to perfecting a strong organization among themselves

THE STEAMER "W. B. DANCE," OF THE FORT BENTON PACKET LINE
lying twelve miles above Nebraska City, N.T.; view looking east
From an original pencil drawing made by Granville Stuart, April 26, 1866

FORT BENTON, LOOKING WEST (UP THE RIVER)
from Lookout hill, Choteau county, Montana; made June 9, 1866

to protect their property. The Eastern Montana Protective Association consolidated with the Montana Stock Growers' Association. Robert Ford, President of the Stock Growers' Association called a meeting to be held in Helena August 15th and 16th, 1882, and practically every stockman in the territory was present. The first meeting closed with a membership of one hundred sixty-eight stockmen. The Montana Stock Growers' Association was now one of the most important organizations in the territory.

The winter of 1881-82 was a mild one with scarcely any snow on the range. By the first of September we had twelve thousand head of cattle in our herd. I was in the saddle all winter keeping the cattle from straying off the range and the Indians from coming on.

Predatory animals were quite troublesome especially the large gray timber wolf that surpasses any other animal in sagacity, fleetness of foot, and powers of endurance. Added to these qualities is an insatiable appetite. It is said of him that he can run longer and easier, eat oftener and more, and display more cunning and ferocity in a given length of time than any other known animal. These wolves have a regular organization and travel in bands numbering from ten to twenty or thirty in a pack under the leadership of a dog wolf. To this captain the entire band yield implicit obedience.

When the buffalo were numerous these wolves followed the herds keeping near the cows and calves, watching for a small bunch to become detached from the main herd; then the wolves would separate into three divisions one slipping in between the main herd and the small bunch, the second division under the leadership of the captain would then move straight for the head of their chosen victim while the third division acted as rear guard thus completely surrounding their prey. Those in the lead would attack the muzzle of the animal while the rear guard slipped up and hamstrung him and after that their victim was helpless and easily dragged down and quickly devoured.

The cattle herds were an easy prey for these grizzly marauders as the cattle were afraid of them and ran at sight of one. The wolves being much fleeter and possessing more endurance found it easy to surround a range animal and drag it down. The range cows would fight desperately to protect their young calves but were never a match for even one large wolf, and these wolves are very large weighing one hundred twenty-five to one hundred fifty pounds. They are prolific breeders having as many as ten whelps in a litter. It is next to impossible to get within gunshot on one and almost equally as difficult to trap or poison them. With plenty of cattle on the range they would not touch a dead carcass preferring to kill their own meat. We carried strychnine with us all the time and by putting it in lard and then spreading it on bacon rinds it was a "piece de resistance" for them and we poisoned not a few in that way.

In the summer the cowboys frequently found a den and then there would be great sport roping them and shooting the awkward sprawling whelps with their six shooters. Charlie Russell the cowboy artist has immortalized this sport in one of his paintings.

The wolfer was the successor of the trapper. About the time that the beaver began to be scarce in the streams, men who had followed the avocation of trapping turned their attention to wolfing. Not until about 1866-67 were the skins of the wolf valuable but from that time on there was a good market for the pelts and wolfing became quite an important industry in Montana.

It was a hard and perilous life led by these brave intrepid men but all the more attractive to them because of the dangers encountered. Every tribe of Indians whether hostile or not to other white men was the avowed enemy of the wolfer as they lost many of their dogs from eating of the poison bait. The friendly tribes would on every occasion cut up and destroy his skins or steal his horses "setting him afoot" when the poor wolfer would be obliged to make his way to the nearest trading post without food or blankets. The hostile Indians lurked about waiting for a chance to get his scalp but were very careful not to attack unless the wolfer could be taken unawares or at a very great disadvantage. The Indian learned early in the game to keep well out of range of his deadly rifle. They usually traveled two together for company and for greater safety.

A wolfer's outfit was a pack horse, a saddle horse each, flour, beans, sugar, coffee, and salt; a pair of blankets, a buffalo robe, the best rifle he could procure, a good revolver, plenty of ammunition, a hunting knife and a supply of strychnine. These supplies were purchased in the fall at one of the trading posts and at the first freeze the wolfers took to the plains and did not return until spring.

The most valuable pelts were those of the gray or timber wolf. These wolves spend the summer in pairs on the timbered mountain sides, having their whelps in caves under the large rocks. They subsist on the fawns of the elk and deer with an occasional grouse or rabbit for a change of diet. As soon as it turns cold they collect in large packs, as many as fifty or sixty together, go to the plains and follow the buffalo.

Just after the first freeze the wolfer begins to set his baits: a buffalo would be killed and the meat poisoned. He would then follow on a short distance and repeat the operation. The baits were usually set in a circle but extended over a wide section of open valley and blizzard swept plains and the poor wolfer suffered severely from the cold while attending the baits. As soon as the wolves ate the poisoned meat they would die and the bodies freeze solid. One poisoned carcass would often kill a hundred or more wolves. When a chinook came or a thaw it was necessary to visit the baits often and skin the wolves to prevent the hides from spoiling. These visits to the baits were always attended by much danger from hostile Indians and at times the danger would be so great that the most fearless wolfer dare not venture out and many valuable skins would be lost. Occasionally a chinook or a prolonged warm spell would come at an inopportune time and hundreds of the skins would spoil, causing the loss of almost an entire season's work to the unfortunate wolfer. A good season was very remunerative, often netting from two to three thousand dollars.

The money rarely did him much good as the wolfer usually came to a trading post, disposed of his skins, and then joined in a wild carousal, drinking and gambling until the money was all gone. Then he would chop wood for the steamboats, hire out to freighters or engage in some work about the fort until winter, when he would again return to the old life of peril and privation.

The wolfer's lines of bait extended from far up into Canada to Colorado and Nebraska. Their principal trading posts were Fort Peck, Fort Benton, Fort Hawley, Fort Brown, the Crow Agency, Fort Pease, and Bozeman.

The Cattle Business

The winter of 1882-83 was a mild one and spring came early with plenty of moisture. The grass was fine. The bounty placed on wolves and coyotes made wolfing profitable once more and the wolfers were rapidly clearing the ranges of those pests. The Canadian Indians were keeping north of the line and our own Indians were slightly less troublesome. All this promised an era of prosperity to the cattle industry but there were still some dark clouds hovering on the horizon.

The sheepmen had discovered that if Montana was not exactly "a land of milk and honey" it was a mighty good grass land and several large bands of sheep were brought on the range. Herds of from two thousand to five thousand head of cattle were being gathered in Texas and New Mexico ready to start for "the land of promise" in the early spring.

The railroads had invaded Montana destroying the Missouri river transportation and the abandoned wood yards furnished splendid rendezvous for horse thieves and cattle rustlers, who were becoming so numerous and so well organized that they threatened to destroy the cattle business.

A meeting of the Montana Stock Growers' Association was called to convene at Miles City on April 17, 1883. This meeting was a memorable one. There were two hundred seventy-nine members present. The town was gaily decorated with bunting and banners and the citizens turned out in mass to welcome the cattlemen. There was a big parade headed by the mayor of the city, and a brass band and the town was thrown wide open to the visitors. The streets were thronged with cowboys dressed in their best with picturesque paraphernalia, and riding the best horses that the country afforded.

This meeting was not all parade and social enjoyment. There were conditions facing the stock growers that called for serious consideration anyone of which if not controlled, threatened the very life of the industry. First and foremost were the "rustlers." It had come to be almost impossible to keep a team or saddle horse on a ranch unless one slept in the manger with a rifle. Our detectives pursued and brought back stolen property and caused the arrest of the thieves and we hired counsel to assist the county attorneys to prosecute them but all to no purpose. The thieves managed to evade the law and became bolder each season.

The experienced cattle men worked unceasingly at this meeting. They gathered the stock laws of our western states and territories and the rules and regulations of other associations and from these were culled and arranged, by a committee of experts, assisted by able counsel, such parts as suited our locality and circumstances, and gave the best satisfaction when in force. Everything was done to bring about better conditions for the stock interests.

With hundreds of thousands of cattle valued at $25,000,000.00 scattered over an area of fifty-eight thousand square miles of territory, it was apparent to the most casual observer that there must be the closest coöperation between the companies if we were to succeed, as what benefited one, must benefit all. From this time on the entire range business was under the direction and control of the Montana Stock Growers' Association and the business run as one large outfit.

At this meeting it was agreed to employ one man in each county as a detective whose duty it would be to track up rustlers and horse thieves and do all in his power to have them arrested and brought to trial. These detectives were to be paid by the Stock Growers' Association.

Minutes of roundup meeting held at "D-S" ranch, Fort Maginnis range May 29, 1883.

Present, Granville Stuart of Davis, Hauser and Co., A. J. Clark of Kohrs and Bielenburg, Horace Brewster for Robert Coburn, Henry Sieben, Robert Clark for N. J. Dovenspeck, Amos Snyder for Snyder and McCauley, John Milliren for Adolph Baro.

It was moved and carried that every stock owner have one vote for each rider furnished and employed by him on this range and that all persons having one thousand or less cattle on the range be required to furnish one rider, or in lieu thereof pay the roundup fund $2.00 per head for branding and marking their calves, that being the price fixed for branding and marking calves for those not attending. All owners having more than one thousand cattle on the range must furnish one rider for each one thousand head or fraction of five hundred or over.

W. C. Burnett was nominated for captain of the roundup for 1883 and was unanimously elected with pay at the rate of $2.50 per day from beginning to close of the roundup.

It was decided to send three men to the lower Musselshell to the Ryan Brothers roundup to work with them and to bring back any cattle from their range found there, with instructions to brand and mark any calves. It was also decided to send two men to Fergus's range when their roundup begins to brand and bring back any cattle from this range found there.

It was decided that one man tally all calves branded and whose duty it shall be to see that there is turned out by their respective owners seven bull calves to each one hundred heifer calves. Henry Sieben was elected to attend to same.

It was also decided to elect a committee of three to inspect the bulls at each corral and to decide upon such as are too old to be of service and order them to be castrated. The owner of each bull so disposed of is required to turn out a bull calf in its place, and said committee shall count all bulls on the range and keep a tally of each brand. Horace Brewster, Henry Sieben, and A. J. Clark were elected committee on bulls.

The spring roundup is to begin on the north side of the range May 30, 1883. It was decided to begin the fall calf roundup Sept. 1, 1883, and the beef roundup to begin Oct. 1, 1883, on the north side of the range. It was decided to pay the day and night herders and the wood haulers out of the roundup funds, and the representatives sent to other ranges were also to be paid out of that fund.

GRANVILLE STUART
SEC.

We had now increased our herd to twelve thousand head of range cattle and were buying thoroughbred bulls of short horn breed to grade them up. None of our cattle were Texas long horns all being a good grade of range stock from Idaho and Oregon.

There was now, on the Fort Maginnis range, twelve outfits, – The Davis-Hauser-Stuart, the Kohrs and Bielenburg, Robert Coburn, Henry Sieben, N. J. Dovenspeck, N. W. McCaulley, C. D. Duncan, Stuart-Anderson, W. C. and G. P. Burnett, F. E. Lawrence, Adolph Baro, and Amos Snyder.

There were also twelve outfits on the Cone butte and Moccasin range: James Fergus and Son, Robert S. Hamilton, The Judith Cattle Co., Tingley Brothers, John H. Ming, Pat Dunlevy, James Dempsey, Chas. Ranges, A. Hash, C. H. Christ, J. L. Stuart, Edward Regan. From this time on the two ranges worked together in one roundup and usually held their meeting and made the start from the "D-S" ranch.

It was a novel sight to witness the big spring roundup pull out. Early in the morning the big horse herd would be driven in and each man would catch and saddle his mount. There was a number of horses that would buck and a lot of half broken colts to ride that would cause a certain amount of excitement. The horse herder in charge of the horse wranglers would lead off in the direction of the objective corral followed by the white covered four-horse chuck wagons, and then the troop of cowboys with their gay handkerchiefs, fine saddles, and silver mounted bridles and spurs.

At the "D-S" ranch there was usually an impromptu dance the night before and there would be quite a gathering of ladies to watch the start. Often they would ride to the first corral to watch the branding and have lunch at the chuck wagon.

A roundup on the range is in charge of the captain absolutely. Every man, whether owner of the largest herd or a humble roustabout, takes his orders from the captain. There were very few orders given, every man knew what he was expected to do and did it.

Work began very early in the morning. The cook was up, breakfast ready and the horse herd in as soon as it was daylight. The riders caught up their horses and saddled them and were ready to start. The men were divided into groups. The circle riders started out two together in every direction and drove to the corral all the cattle that they could find. At the corral the cattle to be branded would be cut out of the bunches and the ropers would catch and throw them. There were wrestlers and the men with the branding irons in the corral to brand and mark. Occasionally an animal would get on "the fight" and make things interesting but the rope horses were as clever as the men about keeping out of danger and rarely ever did we have a serious accident. The work at the corrals was hard and fast. The dust and heat and smell of singeing hair was stifling while the bellowing of the cattle was a perfect bedlam. At the close of the day everyone was tired and ready to roll in his blankets for a night's rest.

The spring or calf roundup usually lasted from four to six weeks. As soon as it was over the hay would have to be put up at the home ranch, range cabins built or put in repair, corrals put in shape, and stray horses gathered. If the herd was being increased we tried to get the new cattle on the range not later than September first. The fall calf roundup started about October 1, and usually required four weeks. After that was the beef roundup, the most important one of all.

The fall of 1883 we shipped from Custer on the Northern Pacific and had a drive of one hundred twenty miles. Cattle must be driven slowly and allowed to graze as they go and yet they must have water regularly. They were as wild as antelope and it required eternal vigilance to keep them from stampeding and running all the fat off. The slightest unusual sight or sound would start them off pell mell.

I well remember one night on the drive. It had been storming all day, rain mixed with snow, and a cold raw wind blowing from the northeast. Our tent blew over and the cook prepared supper over a soggy smoky fire. We were camped on a branch of McDonald creek. There was a steep cut bank on one side of the herd and cut bank coulees in every direction besides prairie dog towns which are full of holes and little mounds of loose earth. The cattle were cold and restless but they were finally bedded down. We ate our supper in the cold and wet. The night herd went on duty and the rest of us unrolled our tarpaulins and turned in. I could hear the cattle moving and occasionally their horns striking together. The boys on guard kept up their monotonous singing.

About eleven o'clock something startled the herd. Instantly every animal was on its feet and the tramping of flying hoofs and rattling horns sounded like artillery. The herders were with the stampede and in an instant every man was in the saddle after them. The night was pitch dark and there was nothing to guide us but the thunder of hoofs. They must be stopped and the only way to do it was to get ahead of them and turn the leaders so that the herd would move in a circle; "milling" it is called. Through the rain and mud and pitch dark, up and down banks and over broken ground, they all went in a mad rush, but the boys succeeded in holding the herd.

Every man had risked his life and some were in the saddle twenty-four hours before they were relieved, but there was not one word of complaint and not one of them thought of his own safety or of leaving the herd so long as his services were needed.

Our beef herd this year was in charge of William C. Burnett, a young Texan, the best range foreman that I ever met. He knew the business from A to Z, and understood the psychology of range cattle and cowboys. The herd reached the Yellowstone, crossed the river, and were loaded and shipped to Chicago where they arrived in first class condition.

Here I wish to give my impression of cowboys or "cowpunchers" as they called themselves, gathered from my ten years association with them on the range. They were a class by themselves and the genuine "dyed in the wool" ones came from the southwest, most of them from Texas. Born and raised on those great open ranges, isolated from everything but cattle they came to know and understand the habits and customs of range cattle as no one else could know them. Always on the frontier beyond organized society or law, they formulated laws of their own that met their requirements, and they enforced them, if necessary, at the point of the six shooter. They were reluctant to obey any law but their own and chafed under restraint. They were loyal to their outfit and to one another. A man that was not square could not long remain with an outfit.

A herd was perfectly safe in the hands of a "boss" and his outfit. Every man would sacrifice his life to protect the herd. If personal quarrels or disputes arose while on a roundup or on a drive, the settlement of the same was left until the roundup was over and the men released from duty, and then they settled their differences man to man and without interference from their comrades. They often paid the penalty with their lives.

Cowpunchers were strictly honest as they reckoned honesty but they did not consider it stealing to take anything they could lay hands on from the government or from Indians. There was always a bitter enmity between them and soldiers.

A shooting scrape that resulted in the death of one or both of the combatants was not considered a murder but an affair between themselves. If a sheriff from Texas or Arizona arrived on one of our northern ranges to arrest a man for murder, the other cowpunchers would invariably help him make his escape.

They were chivalrous and held women in high esteem and were always gentlemen in their presence. They wore the best clothes that they could buy and took a great pride in their personal appearance and in their trapping. The men of our outfit used to pay $25.00 a pair for made-to-order riding boots when the best store boots in Helena were $10.00 a pair.

Their trappings consisted of a fine saddle, silver mounted bridle, pearl-handled six shooter, latest model cartridge belt with silver buckle, silver spurs, a fancy quirt with silver mountings, a fine riata sometimes made of rawhide, a pair of leather chaps, and a fancy hat-band often made from the dressed skin of a diamond-backed rattlesnake. They wore expensive stiff-brimmed light felt hats, with brilliantly colored silk handkerchiefs knotted about their necks, light colored shirts and exquisitely fitted very high heeled riding boots.

Each cowpuncher owned one or more fine saddle horses, often a thoroughbred, on which he lavished his affections, and the highest compliments he could pay you was to allow you to ride his favorite horse. Horse racing was one of his favorite sports.

There were men among them who were lightning to draw a gun, and the best shots that I ever saw; others that could do all the fancy turns with a rope and others that could ride any horse that could be saddled or bridled; but the best and most reliable men were those who did all these things reasonably well.

On the range or the trail their work was steady, hard, and hazardous and with a good deal of responsibility. They were out from three to six months at a time, so when they did get to town it is not to be wondered at if they did do a little celebrating in their own way. Few of them drank to excess, some of them gambled, they all liked a good show and a dance and they always patronized the best restaurant or eating place in town and ice cream and fresh oysters were never omitted from their menu.

When on night herd it was necessary to sing to the cattle to keep them quiet. The sound of the boys' voices made the cattle know that their protectors were there guarding them and this gave them a sense of security. There were two songs that seemed to be favorites. The tunes were similar and all their tunes were monotonous and pitched to a certain key. I suppose they learned just the tune that was most soothing to the cattle. I know that their songs always made me drowsy and feel at peace with the world.

The first place they struck for in a town was the livery stable where they saw to it that their horses were properly cared for, and the barber shop was their next objective. The noisy fellow in exaggerated costume that rode up and down the streets whooping and shooting in the air was never a cowpuncher from any outfit. He was usually some "would be" bad man from the East decked out in paraphernalia from Montgomery, Ward's of Chicago.

As the country settled up and the range business became a thing of the past most of the old reliable cowboys engaged in other business. Their natural love of animals and an out of doors life led many of them to settle on ranches, and they are today among our most successful ranchers and cattle growers.

During the summer of 1882 Carpenter and Robertson moved three thousand stock cattle from Nebraska and located on the Rosebud. The Niobrara Cattle Company drove in ten thousand head of Oregon cattle and located them on Powder river. Scot and Hanks drove in a herd from Nevada and located on the Little Powder river.

In 1879 Robert E. Strahorn published a pamphlet called *Resources of Montana and Attractions of Yellowstone Park,* in which he gave interviews with prominent men and bankers, calling attention to the wonderful opportunities offered in Montana for range cattle business.

Following this came General Brisbin's book, *The Beef Bonanza* in which he pictured in glowing colors the wonderful possibilities of the range cattle business in Montana. The fame of Montana ranges had gone abroad. Eastern papers and magazines published all sorts of romantic tales about the ease and rapidity with which vast fortunes were being accumulated by the "cattle kings."

Profits were figured at one hundred per cent and no mention made of severe winters, storms, dry parched summer ranges, predatory animals, hostile Indians, and energetic "rustlers," or the danger of overstocking the ranges.

The business was a fascinating one and profitable so long as the ranges were not overstocked. The cattlemen found ways to control the other difficulties but the ranges were free to all and no man could say, with authority, when a range was overstocked.

In the summer of 1883 Conrad Kohrs drove in three thousand cattle and placed them on the Sun river range, and D. A. G. Floweree drove three thousand Texas cattle in and threw them on the Sun river range. The Green Mountain Cattle Company drove in twenty-two hundred and located on Emmel's creek. The Dehart Land and Cattle Company came in with two herds of three thousand each and located on the Rosebud. Griffin Brothers and Ward drove in three thousand head and located on the Yellowstone. J. M. Holt came in with three thousand head and located on Cabin creek. Tusler and Kempton brought in three herds of twenty-five hundred each and located on Tongue river. Ryan Brothers brought in three herds of three thousand each and located on the Musselshell. John T. Murphy and David Fratt drove in six thousand head and located on the Musselshell. Poindexter and Orr increased their herds in Madison county. Lepley brought in two thousand head, Green three thousand head and Conley twenty-five hundred and placed them on the range near Fort Benton. These cattle were nearly all Texas cattle and came up over the Texas trail. By the first of October there were six hundred thousand head of range cattle in the territory and these together with the horses and sheep was as much stock as the ranges could safely carry.

There was never, in Montana, any attempt on the part of the large cattle companies to keep out small owners, homesteaders, or permanent settlers. On the contrary every possible assistance was given to the settlers by the larger companies.

It was customary to allow settlers to milk range cows, provided they let the calves have a share of the milk and we frequently purchased the butter from the homesteader, paying him fifty cents a pound for it. The company would lend horses and farm machinery, employ the men and recover stolen horses and cattle at times when it would have been utterly impossible for a lone rancher to do so. One instance to illustrate. A settler on our range had the misfortune to break his leg and while he lay helpless in his cabin thieves drove off his span of fine mares. Cowboys immediately started in pursuit, recovered the mares and kept them at the ranch until the owner was able to look after them himself. Had they not done so the thieves would have crossed the British line and been safely in Canada before the authorities could have been notified and the team would have been irretrievably lost.

The large companies encouraged schools and their taxes largely supported them. On our range whenever as many as six children could be assembled I provided a good log school house and a six months' term of school each year. The cowboys on the range saw to it that the teacher, if a young woman, was provided with a good saddle horse and not allowed to become lonely.

At the ranch I had a library of three thousand volumes and we subscribed for the leading newspapers and magazines. At the James Fergus' ranch on Armell's creek, there was another splendid library and the leading periodicals. These books were at the disposal of everybody.

Few of the cattle outfits had any money invested in land nor did they attempt to fence or control large bodies of land. The land on the ranges was unsurveyed and titles could not be had. The cattleman did not want to see fences on the range as during severe storms the cattle drifted for miles and if they should strike a fence they were likely to drift against it and perish with the cold.

In the days of the big ranges there was never any serious trouble between the cattlemen and the sheepmen and there was never a "range war" between them in Montana. Many of the cattlemen also had bands of sheep.

It would be impossible to make persons not present on the Montana cattle ranges realize the rapid change that took place on those ranges in two years. In 1880 the country was practically uninhabited. One could travel for miles without seeing so much as a trapper's bivouac. Thousands of buffalo darkened the rolling plains. There were deer, antelope, elk, wolves, and coyotes on every hill and in every ravine and thicket. In the whole territory of Montana there were but two hundred and fifty thousand head of cattle, including dairy cattle and work oxen.

In the fall of 1883 there was not one buffalo remaining on the range and the antelope, elk, and deer were indeed scarce. In 1880 no one had heard tell of a cowboy in "this niche of the woods" and Charlie Russell had made no pictures of them; but in the fall of 1883 there were six hundred thousand head of cattle on the range. The cowboy, with leather chaps, wide hats, gay handkerchiefs, clanking silver spurs, and skin fitting high heeled boots was no longer a novelty but had become an institution. Small ranches were being taken by squatters along all the streams and there were neat and comfortable log school houses in all the settlements.

The story of the Montana cattle ranges would not be complete without a brief description of the Texas trail, as more than one half of the Montana range cattle were driven over that trail and almost every cowboy that worked on the ranges made one or more drives up the trail.

The trail started at the Rio Grande, crossing the Colorado river at San Angelo, then across the Llanos Estacado, or Staked Plains to the Red river about where Amarillo now is. From there it ran due north to the Canadian river and on to Dodge City where it crossed the Arkansas river and then on to Ogalalla, crossing the North Platte at Camp Clark. From Ogalalla it followed the Sidney and Black hills stage road north to Cottonwood creek, then to Hat creek and across to Belle Fourche, then over to Little Powder river and down that stream to its mouth where it crossed Tongue river to the Yellowstone, crossing that stream just above Fort Keogh. From here it ran up Sunday creek across the Little Dry, following up the Big Dry to the divide, then down Lodge Pole creek to the Musselshell river which was the end of the trail. Texas cattle were sometimes driven clear up into Canada but never in any considerable numbers. Ogalalla was a great trading center in the range days. Many herds were driven up from Texas, sold, and turned over to northern buyers, at that place.

There were usually from two to three thousand cattle in a trail herd, and the outfit consisted of a trail boss, eight cowpunchers, a cook, a horse wrangler, about sixty-five cow horses, and a four-horse chuck wagon that carried provisions and the men's blankets. The food provided was corn meal, sorghum molasses, beans, salt, sugar, and coffee.

The cattle were as wild as buffalo and difficult to handle for the first week or ten days, until they had gained confidence in the cowpunchers and accustomed themselves to the daily routine. By that time some old range steer had established himself leader of the herd and everything settled down to a regular system.

The daily program was breakfast at daylight and allow the herd to graze awhile. The horse herd and mess wagon pulled out and then the herd started, with two cowpunchers in the lead or "point." The man on the left point was next, in command, to the "trail boss," two on the swing, two on the flank, and two drag drivers whose business it was to look after the calves that played out, the footsore and the laggards. In this order they grazed along until noon. The mess wagon would camp; one-half the crew would go in, eat dinner, change horses and go back to the herd as quickly as possible and the other half would eat, change horses and the herd would be started forward again. It would be kept moving until the sun was low and sufficient water for the cattle would be found. Camp would then be made, one half the men would go in to supper, catch up night horses and return to the herd when the remaining half would do the same. The herd would be grazing on bed ground and by dark would all be down.

The nights were divided into four periods. The first watch stood until 10 o'clock, the second until 12 o'clock, the third until 2 A. M. and the fourth until morning. In case of storms or a stampede, the entire crew was on duty and remained with the herd until it was back on the trail again, no matter how long that might be. It was no unusual thing for cowpunchers to remain in the saddle thirty-six hours at a stretch but they never complained and not one of them ever left a herd until relieved. Of all the thousands of herds driven over the Texas trail, there was never one lost or abandoned by the cowpunchers.

When the first herds started north, Indians and Mexican outlaws tried the experiment of slipping up to the herd on a dark night, popping a blanket to stampede it, with the hope of cutting off some of the lead cattle and driving them east to a market. The practice did not last long. The dead bodies of a few Indians and Mexicans found on the plains, told the story and was sufficient warning to others similarly minded. The cowpunchers were loyal to their outfit and would fight for it quicker than they would for themselves.

One of the worst things that they had to contend with on the trail was the terrific electrical storms so prevalent on the plains, and along the Arkansas and Platte rivers during the summer months. They came on suddenly with a high wind that blew the tent over and the chuck wagon too, if it was not staked to the ground. Zigzag streaks of lightning tore through the inky blackness of the sky, followed by deafening claps of thunder that fairly made the ground tremble. Over and around the herd the lightning was always worst. Every man in the outfit is out in the darkness and pouring rain, riding around the cattle, singing their weird cowboy songs in an effort to keep the herd quiet. Two of their favorites were "We go North in the Spring but will return in the Fall," and "We are bound to follow the Lone Star Trail." All at once comes a flash and a crash and a bolt strikes in the midst of them. It is too much. The cattle spring to their feet as one animal. There is a rattling of horns and thunder of hoofs as the maddened herd dashes off across the slippery broken ground and the men riding at breakneck speed to keep ahead of and turn them; for the only way to stop them is to throw them in a circle and "mill" them. If a horse should fall it was certain death to horse and rider and not a few lost their lives in that way.

In the morning the herd might be fifteen or twenty miles from camp and it would take all day or longer to get them on the trail again and all the cowpunchers would be kept in the saddle without rest or food until all were moving along again. If a cowboy was killed in a stampede his comrades dug a shallow grave, wrapped the trampled form in his blankets and laid him to rest.

The greatest responsibility rested on the trail boss.

He had to know where water was a day ahead and the drive made according. There was one dry drive forty miles long. When there was a long dry drive the cattle would be watered and then pushed on away into the night. Cattle can smell water for a very long distance and if the wind was from the north next morning, the herd would travel along all right, but if there was no wind they would travel slow. If the wind blew up from behind late in the afternoon when they were suffering for water there was trouble. They would "bull," that is try to turn and go back to water and it required all the skill and best efforts of every cowpuncher in the outfit to keep the herd moving forward and then it could not always be done.

I have seen a herd traveling along only a few miles from where they were going in to water, when the wind would suddenly blow from a river behind them. The cattle would turn as one cow, start for that water, possibly ten miles distant, and nothing could stop them.

A herd cannot be made to swim a large river if the sunshine on the water reflects in their eyes; nor will they go into a river if the wind is blowing and the water ripples. In 1885 John Lea, one of the experienced trail bosses, struck the Yellowstone river with a herd. The wind blew hard for three days and kept the water rippled, and nothing would induce those cattle to cross the river until the water was smooth.

A day's drive on the trail is from ten to fifteen miles, but it is always governed by water. A herd of steers make much better time than a mixed herd. There was never any such thing as "resting up" or "laying over;" the herd was kept moving forward all the time.

A company or an individual stocking range, would go south, buy the cattle and notify his foreman to send an outfit to some point south to receive a herd of cattle and to trail them to somewhere in Montana, and give him the brands and money for expenses. There was a fortune in that herd of cattle but he was not worried. He knew the cattle would arrive on time and in the best possible condition. While in St. Louis in 1884, a friend of mine told me that he had just bought three thousand two-year old steers in Texas for his range on the Musselshell. I asked him if he was going south to come up with the drive.

"H—l, no!" was the reply. "I am going to Miles City and play poker and be comfortable until those steers arrive." And that is just what he did and the herd was on the Musselshell in August and the steers were fat enough for beef.

Trailing cattle came to be a profession and the trail men a distinct class. They came north with a herd in the spring and returned south in the fall, worked in the chaparral, gathering another herd during the winter and then drove north again in the spring. They took a great pride in their work and were never so happy as when turning a fine herd on the range at the end of the trail.

It was a pleasing sight to see a herd strung out on the trail. The horses and the white-covered mess wagon in the lead, followed by a mass of sleek cattle a half mile long; the sun flashing on their bright horns and on the silver conchos, bridles, spurs, and pearl-handled six shooters of the cowpunchers. The brilliant handkerchiefs knotted about their necks furnished the needed touch of color to the picture.

Cattle Rustlers and Vigilantes

At the close of the fall roundup (1883) our tallies showed that we had suffered at least a three per cent loss from "rustling." These thieves were splendidly organized and had established headquarters and had enough friends among the ranchers to enable them to carry on their work with perfect safety.

Near our home ranch we discovered one rancher whose cows invariably had twin calves and frequently triplets, while the range cows in that vicinity were nearly all barren and would persist in hanging around this man's corral, envying his cows their numerous children and bawling and lamenting their own child-less fate. This state of affairs continued until we were obliged to call around that way and threaten to hang the man if his cows had any more twins.

The "rustlers" were particularly active along the Missouri and Yellowstone rivers and our neighbors in the Dakota bad lands were great sufferers. A meeting of stockmen was called at Helena on October 16 to consider what best to do. The first thing necessary was to discover the leaders and to locate their rendezvous. It was then decided to bring the matter before the Stock Growers' Association at the regular spring meeting.

The second annual meeting of The Montana Stock Growers' Association convened at Miles City on April 20, 1884. There were four hundred and twenty-nine stockmen present. The citizens' welcome was as cordial as it had been the previous year and the same splendid entertainment offered, but the meeting itself was not the harmonious gathering that the previous meeting had been. Everybody seemed to have a grievance. The members of the association that had been members of the legislature the previous year came in for their full share of censure. We were blamed for everything that had happened but the good weather.

The matters for consideration were overstocking the ranges, the dread pleuro-pneumonia, or Texas fever, that was claiming such heavy toll in Kansas and Nebraska and how to put a stop to "rustling."

The civil laws and courts had been tried and found wanting. The Montana cattlemen were as peaceable and law-abiding a body of men as could be found anywhere but they had $35,000,000 worth of property scattered over seventy-five thousand square miles of practically uninhabited country and it must be protected from thieves. The only way to do it was to make the penalty for stealing so severe that it would lose its attractions. When the subject was brought up some of the members were for raising a small army of cowboys and raiding the country: but the older and more conservative men knew that that would never do.

I openly opposed any such move and pointed out to them that the "rustlers" were strongly fortified, each of their cabins being a miniature fortress. They were all armed with the most modern weapons and had an abundance of ammunition, and every man of them was a desperado and a dead shot. If we had a scrap with them the law was on the side of the "rustlers." A fight with them would result in the loss of many lives and those that were not killed would have to stand trial for murder in case they killed any of the "rustlers." My talk did not have the conciliatory effect that I expected

and seemed only to add fuel to the fire. The younger
men felt that they had suffered enough at the hand of
thieves and were for "cleaning them out" no matter
what the cost.

The Marquis DeMores, who was a warm personal
friend of mine and with whom I had had some previous
talks on the subject, was strongly in favor of a "rustlers'
war" and openly accused me of "backing water." The
Marquis was strongly supported by Theodore Roose-
velt, who was also a member of the Montana Stock
Growers' Association from Dakota. In the end the
conservative members of the association carried the day
and it was voted that the association would take no
action against the "rustlers." In some way the "rustlers" got information about what was done at the meeting and were jubilant. They returned to their favorite
haunts and settled down to what promised to be an era
of undisturbed and successful operations.

While we were absent on the roundup, a party came
to the ranch, stole a valuable stallion and a number of
other good horses. Another party collected twenty-
four head of beef steers from the Moccasin range and
attempted to drive them north of the line into Canada;
but when they found they could not evade the range
riders, drove the cattle into a coulee and killed them,
leaving the carcasses to spoil.

At the close of the roundup there was a meeting of a
few stockmen at the "D-S" ranch. They and some men
employed by the Stock Growers' Association had been
watching the operations of the rustlers. The captain
of this band of outlaws was John Stringer who answered to the sobriquet of "Stringer Jack." He was
a tall handsome young fellow, well educated, and of a
pleasing personality. His distinguishing features were

his piercing gray eyes, white even teeth, and pleasant smile. He came to Montana in 1876 and hunted buffalo along the Missouri and Yellowstone rivers and was a conspicuous figure around the wood yards, trading posts, and military cantonments. He did not drink to excess but was an inveterate gambler. When the buffalo were gone he turned his attention to rustling cattle and stealing horses and established his headquarters on the Missouri river at the mouth of the Pouchette.

There were rustlers' rendezvous at the mouth of the Musselshell, at Rocky Point and at Wolf Point. J. A. Wells had a herd of cattle on the Judith river in charge of a herder who had eight saddle horses. On the twenty-fifth of June, Narciss Lavardure and Joe Vardner came up the river and camped opposite the Well's camp. Next day the herder crossed the river to look for some stray stock and as soon as he was out of sight Vardner and Lavardure crossed the river and drove off the seven saddle horses. They were going up Eagle creek on the run when they accidentally met William Thompson, who knew the horses and ordered them to stop. Lavardure answered by turning and firing at Thompson but his horse plunged and he missed his mark. Thompson, who was well armed and riding a good horse, gave chase. He shot and fatally wounded Vardner and after a race of six miles, captured Lavardure and brought him and the horses back to the Well's camp. Thompson and his prisoner were taken across the river in a skiff and the latter placed in a stable under guard. At 2 A. M. on the morning of the twenty-seventh the guard was overpowered by an armed posse and Lavardure was taken out and hanged.

Sam McKenzie, a Scotch half-breed, had spent two

MAIDEN, MONTANA, IN THE JUDITH MOUNTAINS, JULY 1, 1885
From an old photograph in the Granville Stuart papers

years around old Fort Hawley on the Missouri river under pretense of being a wolfer but in reality was one of the most active horse thieves. He stole horses in Montana, drove them across the line into Canada, sold them, then stole horses up there and brought them back and sold them around Benton. He had been very successful in dodging the authorities on both sides of the line because of his many friends among the Cree half-breeds in Canada and in the Judith basin. On July 3, McKenzie was caught in a cañon a few miles above Fort Maginnis with two stolen horses in his possession and that night he was hanged from the limb of a cottonwood tree, two miles below the fort.

Early in June two suspicious characters came into the Judith basin with a small band of horses with a variety of brands on them and among them two fairly good "scrub" race horses. Word of their suspicious appearance and actions came to us and we telegraphed to several places to try to find out who the men were and whence they came.

I first met them on July 3, while out range riding, when I accidentally came on their camp at a spring just above Nelson's ranch (The old overland post office). The men were as tough looking characters as I have ever met, especially Owen who had long unkept black hair, small, shifty, greenish gray eyes and a cruel mouth. "Rattle Snake Jake," despite his bad sounding sobriquet, was not quite so evil looking as his pal, although he was far from having a prepossessing appearance. Both men were armed, each wearing two forty-four Colt revolvers and a hunting knife. When I rode into their camp, Fallon was sitting on a roll of blankets cleaning a Winchester rifle. Owen was reclining against a stump smoking and another Winchester lay on a coat within easy reach. Owen was self-possessed, almost insolent, "Rattle Snake Jake" was civil but nervously tinkered with the gun and kept his eyes on me all the time I was in their camp. I knew that they were a bad lot but had nothing to cause their arrest at that time, but decided to keep an eye on them while they were on the range.

On the morning of July 4 Ben Cline came along the road with a race horse on his way to Lewistown. "Rattle Snake Jake" saw the horse and challenged Cline for a race. Cline did not want to race, giving as his reason that he had his horse matched against a gray mare to run at the races at Lewistown and wanted to get his horse over there in good condition. After a little bantering on the part of Fallon a race was arranged between one of his horses and Cline's for fifty dollars a side, and a level stretch of road almost in front of Nelson's house selected for the race course. Owen bet ten dollars on the Fallon horse with one of Cline's companions. The Cline horse won the race and Cline and his companions resumed their interrupted journey to Lewistown.

Shortly after Cline and his friends left, Owen and Fallon packed up their belongings and set out for Lewistown. At this time Lewistown was just a small village, but they were having a Fourth of July celebration and people from a hundred miles in every direction had flocked to the town, to take part in the festivities.

Owen and "Rattle Snake Jake" arrived in town about one P. M., rode up to Crowley's saloon, dismounted, went in and had several drinks and then rode on to the race track. Here they joined the throng around the track but took no part in the betting until almost the last race when they bet quite heavily and lost their money. This, together with a few drinks of bad whiskey, put them in an ugly mood.

A young man by the name of Bob Jackson, dressed in costume, representing Uncle Sam, rode in the parade and afterwards was at the race track, still wearing the grotesque costume. For some unaccountable reason his presence near Owen gave that gentleman offense and he struck Jackson over the head with the butt of his revolver, felling him to the ground; then placing a cocked revolver to Jackson's head, compelled him to crawl in the dust like a snake. Owen then turned to "Rattle Snake Jake" and said, "Well I guess we will clean out this town" and at that shot at random into the crowd, but fortunately did not hit anybody.

The desperadoes mounted their horses and rode back to the saloon where they each had more drinks: then flourishing their revolvers in a threatening way and cursing and swearing declared that they intended to clean up the town, swaggered out into the street.

Quite a number of men who had been at the race track, sensing trouble hurried back to town, went to Power's store and armed themselves with Winchesters and took up positions in the buildings on either side of the street. Out in the street "Rattle Snake Jake" mounted his horse and Owen started to mount his, when he spied Joe Doney standing in front of Power's store. Revolver in hand he started to cross the street. When within a few feet of the walk Doney pulled a twenty-two caliber revolver and shot him in the stomach. A second shot struck Owen's hand, causing him to drop his revolver.

Doney ran into the store. Owen quickly recovered his revolver and fired at Doney just as he disappeared

inside the door. The men in the store answered the
shot with their Winchesters and Owen retreated up the
street toward a tent occupied by a photographer.
"Rattle Snake Jake," revolver in hand started to ride
up the street in the opposite direction, when a shot fired
by someone in the saloon, struck him in the side. He
kept on for a short distance when his cartridge belt fell
to the ground and he drew up to recover it. Looking
back he saw that Owen was not following him but was
wounded and could not get away, and turning his
horse he rode back to his comrade through a perfect
shower of lead coming from both sides of the street
and together the two men made their last stand in front
of the tent.

The citizens in the store and saloons and from behind
buildings kept up their firing, while the two desperadoes standing exposed to their merciless fire, coolly
and deliberately answered shot for shot, emptied and
re-loaded their guns and emptied them again until
they could no longer pull a trigger.

Two young men, Benjamin Smith and Joseph Jackson, were crossing an open space a short distance from
the tent when "Rattle Snake Jake" caught sight of them.
and dropping down on one knee took careful aim and
fired on them. The first shot grazed Jackson's cheek
and the second one pierced his hat and took a lock of his
hair. The third one lodged in Smith's brain, killing
him instantly.

A few minutes later Owen reached for his rifle,
pitched forward and fell to the ground and almost at
the same moment a bullet struck "Rattle Snake Jake"
in the breast and he dropped. As soon as both men
were down the citizens ceased firing but the bandits
continued with their revolvers so long as conscious-

ness remained. When the smoke of battle cleared away examination of the bodies showed that "Rattle Snake Jake" had received nine wounds and Owen eleven, anyone of which would have proved fatal.

In the evening Judge Toombs held an inquest over the bodies, the photographer, in front of whose tent they were killed, took their pictures and then they were given burial on a little knoll on the Pichette ranch.

On the afternoon of July 4, a telegram came to me from Buffalo, Wyoming, stating that Charles Fallon, alias "Rattle Snake Jake," and Edward Owen, were desperate characters and were wanted at several places. The two men had spent the winter on Powder river at the mouth of Crazy Woman, gambling, horse racing, and carousing. On their way north they had stolen some good horses from John R. Smith's ranch near Trabing, Wyoming, and traded them to the Crow Indians. Later on we learned that Owen was from Shreveport, Louisiana, and was wanted there for killing a negro. Charles Fallon hailed from Laredo on the Texas border and was wanted in New Mexico for shooting up a ranch and burning buildings and hay stacks.

Billy Downs was located at one of the wood yards on the Missouri at the mouth of the Musselshell, ostensibly to trap wolves, but in reality to sell whiskey to the Indians. His place soon came to be headquarters for tough characters, and it was but a short time until Downs himself was stealing horses and killing cattle. Downs was a married man and his wife was at the wood yard with him. Because of sympathy for the woman, he was warned that he was being watched and that if he did not change his tactics he was sure to get into trouble. He paid not the least attention to the warning, but continued to surround himself with the worst characters on the river and kept on stealing horses and killing cattle.

On the night of July 4, a committee of vigilantes arrived at the Downs' place and called on him to come out. This at first he refused to do but after a short parley he did come out, accompanied by a notorious character known as California Ed. Both men plead guilty to stealing ponies from the Indians but denied that they had stolen from white men, but they failed to account for the twenty-six horses in the corral, all bearing well-known brands. They claimed that the quantity of dried meat found in the house was dried buffalo meat, notwithstanding the fact that there had not been a buffalo on the range for more than two years. In the stable was a stack of fresh hides folded and salted ready to be shipped down the river, all bearing the brand of the Fergus Stock Co. The two men were taken out to a little grove of trees and hanged.

At the time the vigilante committee started for the mouth of Musselshell, another party left for the vicinity of Rocky Point where two notorious horse thieves, known as Red Mike and Brocky Gallagher, were making their headquarters. They had stolen about thirty head of horses from Smith river, changed the brands and were holding them in the bad lands. They had also been operating over on the Moccasin range and stolen horses from J. H. Ming's ranch and from J. L. Stuart.

When the vigilantes arrived at Rocky Point the men were not there but had crossed over on the north side of the river. The party followed after, and captured them and recovered some of the horses. Both men plead guilty to horse stealing and told their captors that there were six head of the stolen horses at Dutch Louie's ranch on Crooked creek.

Fifteen miles below the mouth of the Musselshell, at an old abandoned wood yard, lived old man James, his two sons, and a nephew. Here also was the favorite haunt of Jack Stringer. There was a log cabin and a stable with a large corral built of logs, connecting the two buildings. One hundred yards from the cabin in a wooded bottom was a tent constructed of poles and covered with three wagon sheets. At the cabin were old man James, his two sons, Frank Hanson and Bill Williams. Occupying the tent were Jack Stringer, Paddy Rose, Swift Bill, Dixie Burr,[116] Orvil Edwards, and Silas Nickerson.

On the morning of July 8, the vigilantes arrived at Bates Point. The men were divided into three parties. Three guarded the tent, five surrounded the cabin and one was left behind with the saddle horses. They then waited for daylight. Old man James was the first to appear. He was ordered to open the corral and drive out the horses. This he did but refused to surrender, backed into the cabin and fired a shot from his rifle through a small port hole at the side of the door. This was followed by a volley from port holes all around the cabin and in an instant the whole party was in action.

Two of the vigilantes crawled up and set fire to the hay stack and the cabin. The men inside stationed themselves at port holes and kept up the fight until they were all killed or burned up. The cabin burned to the ground. The tent was near the river bank and almost

---

[116] According to Sam Stuart, a son of Granville Stuart, Dixie Burr was a son of the well-known F. H. Burr an engineer of Lieutenant Mullan, and long prominent in Montana. He was also a nephew of Granville Stuart. – ED.

surrounded by thick brush and it was easier to escape from it than to get out of the cabin. Stringer Jack crawled under the tent and reached a dense clump of willows from which he made his last stand. Dixie Burr had his arm shattered with a rifle ball but jumped into an old dry well and remained until dark. Paddy Rose ran out of the tent, passed back of the men engaged at the cabin and concealed himself in a small washout and after dark made his escape. Nickerson, Edwards, and Swift Bill reached the river bank and crawling along through the brush and under the bank, succeeded in passing above the men at the cabin and hid in some brush and drift wood. Orvil Edwards and Silas Nickerson were the only ones that escaped without wounds. After the fight at the cabin the men went down the river and spent the day looking for the men who had escaped but failed to find them.

On the afternoon of the ninth, the fugitives rolled some dry logs into the river, constructed a raft and started down stream. At Popular creek agency they were discovered by some soldiers stationed there, ordered to come on shore and were arrested.

Notice of their arrest was sent to Fort Maginnis and Samuel Fischel, deputy U. S. marshall, started at once to get the prisoners and take them to White Sulphur Springs. At the mouth of the Musselshell a posse met Fischel and took the prisoners from him. Nearby stood two log cabins close together. A log was placed between the cabins, the ends resting on the roofs, and the four men were hanged from the log. The cabins caught fire and were burned down and the bodies were cremated.

Paddy Rose lay all day concealed in a little washout in the bad lands and at night struck for Fort Benton, where he had wealthy and influential relatives. With their influence and assistance he succeeded in reaching the Canadian border.

There were one hundred and sixty-five stolen horses recovered at Bates Point and one hundred and nineteen at other places. After the fight at Bates Point the vigilantes disbanded and returned to their respective homes. This clean-up of horse thieves put a stop to horse and cattle stealing in Montana for many years.

Several of the men that met their fate on the Missouri in July, 1884, belonged to wealthy and influential families and there arose a great hue and cry in certain localities over what was termed "the arrogance of the cattle kings." The cattlemen were accused of hiring "gunmen" to raid the country and drive the small ranchers and sheepmen off the range. There was not a grain of truth in this talk.

There were but fourteen members of the vigilance committee and they were all men who had stock on the range and who had suffered at the hands of the thieves. There was not one man taken on suspicion and not one was hanged for a first offense. The men that were taken were members of an organized band of thieves that for more than two years had evaded the law and robbed the range at will. The fact that the stock men loaned milch cows, horses, and farm machinery to settlers on small ranches, branded their calves for them at roundup prices, established schools for them, bought their butter and vegetables at high prices and in every way helped them to get a start is proof that any law-abiding person was welcome in this country.

In 1879, when I located the "D-S" ranch, there were no sheep in that part of the country. In 1884 there were fifty thousand sheep on Salt, Dog, Armell's, Deer,

Box Elder, Black Butte, McDonald, Plumb, and Warm Spring creeks and there never was any trouble between the cattle and sheep men of Montana.

Russel B. Harrison and myself were selected to draft laws and to present them at the next session of the territorial legislature that would protect the cattle interests and make any further action of a vigilantes' committee unnecessary, and after an all session struggle we did succeed in having laws passed which did enable us to protect ourselves in this way.

A board of stock commissioners was created, and a tax levy of one mill on the dollar on the value of all cattle, horses and mules, was made each year, to be expended under the direction of the board of stock commissioners, who were authorized to employ a sufficient number of stock inspectors to inspect all cattle, horses and mules that were being driven or shipped out of the territory of Montana. The same law made it imperative that all stock of that description should be inspected by the employees of the stock commissioners before it could be driven or shipped out. All persons driving or shipping any stock out of the territory were compelled to give to the inspectors a receipt for all stock not carrying their brand. This stock could then be taken to eastern markets and sold by these shippers under the same conditions and prices as their own stock, and the money received had to be turned over to the board of stock commissioners and was by them distributed to the real owners. As an additional safeguard, the shipper was compelled to give a receipt to an inspector where the cattle were sold (usually at Chicago). You will note that the live stock interests paid all the expense, connected with putting a stop to stealing stock off the open range: but it did stop it.

I was elected president of the board of stock commissioners and served in that capacity for seven years until I went to South America.   Almost the entire direction of this immense volume of business fell upon my shoulders.   I received no compensation whatever for these years of work, except the knowledge that my initiative and labors placed the live stock industry of Montana upon a safe and businesslike basis, where it has remained up to the present time.

I say live stock industry of Montana because the vast sheep industry of the state, seeing what results followed proper legislation in the cattlemen's case, soon followed our example and procured authority for a board of sheep commissioners and inspectors and a tax levy on the sheep industry, under which they have greatly prospered unto this day.

The first national convention of cattlemen held in the United States was called together at St. Louis, Missouri, on November 14, 1884.   There were forty-six delegates from Montana and upon our arrival in the city we at once secured a room at the Southern hotel for consultation purposes and organized into a committee to work together.   R. B. Harrison was chosen secretary and I chairman of this committee.

On Monday, November 17, at 10 A. M., the convention assembled in the grand hall of the exposition building and organized.   Three thousand delegates answered roll call.   Every state and territory in the union was represented.

This convention was the greatest meeting of men representing one industry ever held in the United States up to that time.   The three thousand delegates represented the third largest industry in the United States. It resulted in much benefit to stockmen all over the country as it brought together men from every section of the United States and each section became acquainted with the aims and aspirations of other sections and we were enabled to do better work together to our mutual benefit.

Throughout this convention the Montana delegation worked as one man and although we were small in numbers as compared with Texas, Kansas, and the Indian Nation, we were able to make our influence felt in the great convention and to greatly benefit our cattle industry.

The winter of 1884 and 1885 was another ideal one for range stock. There was but little snow and what fell did not lay on the ground but went off with chinook winds: in fact there was not enough snow to supply the cattle with water. We were obliged to keep range riders along some of the streams to cut holes in the ice so that cattle could get water.

Spring came early, March was unseasonably warm, the frost came out of the ground, the new grass started and trees and bushes budded and put forth leaves. Vegetation was as advanced as it usually is in May. There was no rain or snow in March and the drouth continued through April and May. In May we had frequent hot dry winds that shriveled the grass and licked up what little moisture there was. Water holes and small creeks were as dry as they usually are in August. Conditions on the range were serious.

About the twentieth of May, Reverend Van Orsdale,[117] S. S. Hobson and myself were passengers on the coach from Helena to White Sulphur Springs.

[117] Reverend William W. Van Orsdel came to Montana in 1872 as a minister of the Methodist Church. He was one of the most influential and best beloved ministers in the territory. – ED.

Conversation naturally turned to the unusually warm
weather and the continued drouth.   "Brother Van" (as
we all affectionately called the beloved missionary)
was a jovial soul, and after listening to our complaints
and misgivings about the drouth for some time, suggested that we had better quit complaining and pray
for rain.   Hobson and I had both been on the frontier
for a long time and had to confess that we were stronger
on "cussing" than we were on "praying" and we didn't
believe that our prayers would be effective, because it is
written in the Good Book that "The prayers of the
wicked availeth nothing."

We had all been joking but "Brother Van" became
quite serious and after a short silence gravely re-
marked: "Gentlemen, I will pray for rain."

At White Sulphur Springs we separated, Hobson
and I to go to our respective ranches to start the roundup and "Brother Van" to his missionary work.   On
June 2, it began to rain and continued almost without
cessation for three weeks.   The water holes filled,
every little dry creek became a raging torrent and the
large streams were all out of their banks.   There were
not many bridges on the range but the few that were
there washed out.   We worked in rain and mud and
swam creeks and coulees the entire roundup.

There never was such fine grass on the range before.
The bunch grass grew tall and waved in the wind like
fields of grain.   I cannot say that I had much faith in
prayers but I have always credited "Brother Van" with
having a hand in bringing on that rain and saving the
range.

In the spring of 1885 our outfit incorporated for
one million dollars and issued one thousand shares of
stock, par value one hundred dollars per share.   The

name was changed from Stuart, Kohrs, and Co. to the Pioneer Cattle Company.   On the spring roundup we branded twenty-six hundred and twenty-two calves and two thousand and eleven on the fall roundup.   The outlook for a peaceful and prosperous year seemed exceptionally good but we were not left long in this happy delusion.

During the time of and at the close of the Riel Rebellion [118] in Canada, the Indians that were more or less mixed up in that fuss, took refuge south of the line and camped in the heart of the cattle ranges.   Between six and seven hundred Cree Indians, lately in open revolt against the Dominion of Canada, were allowed to move boldly, with their families, to our side of the line and locate, without any means of support and of necessity preying on citizens of Montana.

The presence of this seven hundred families of starving Indians on the range was not the worst feature by any means.   These Indians were connected by blood and tribal relations with our Blackfeet, Bloods, and Gros Ventres as well as with the reservation Indians north of the line.   The Indian agents at our agencies granted their wards permission to leave the reservations on pretense of visiting their relatives, at their pleasure.   Those north of the line came without permission, consequently as soon as the weather was fine the entire eastern portion of Montana swarmed with roving bands of Indians whose only means of subsistence was stealing cattle on the range, and whose only source of amusement was stealing horses.

The few stock detectives that we could employ were powerless in the face of this invading hoard.   Before

118 For account of this rebellion see Alexander Begg, *History of the Northwest* (Toronto, 1894, 3 vols.) vol. i, pp. 373-435. – Ed.

the spring roundup was fairly under way we began to find hides and parts of carcasses of slaughtered animals strewn over the praries. The stage driver reported that on one drive over his route, between Maiden and Big Sandy, a distance of one hundred and twenty miles he had counted six carcasses of cattle that had been killed by Indians and only the choicest meat taken. The rest, together with the hide, was left to spoil.

The president of the Montana Stock Growers' Association sent a letter explaining the situation to the various Indian agents and requested that they do not grant their wards permission to leave their reservations. Very few paid any attention to our request, and when we overhauled some of the reservation Indians they waved their permits in our faces and continued on their way rejoicing.

We next petitioned our commissioner of Indian affairs in Washington to prohibit the issuing of these permits for the Indians to leave the reservation but without results.

Next we asked that some of the troops that were stationed at the various military posts in Montana be distributed at the principal places where these Indians pass, one company of cavalry at each of the following points to wit. The Sweet Grass hills near Milk river, at the Piegan agency at the mouth of Arrow creek, and near the pass at the east end of the Little Snow mountains, thirty miles south of Fort Maginnis. The troops cooped up in military quarters in Montana, shooting forty shots a day at tin Indians on the parade ground were just as anxious to take the field and try their marksmanship on real Indians, as we were to have them; but they were not permitted to move without orders from the commander of the Department of the

Missouri, who was stationed at Fort Snelling, near St. Paul.

After sending petition after petition to the President of the United States, the Department of the Interior, the War Department and then clear down the labyrinth of the military authorities; we were finally granted the privilege of reporting any Indians found on the range, stealing horses or killing cattle, to the nearest military post. Blessed privilege! I will give one incident which will show conclusively what a wonderful assistance and protection this was to the pioneer settler, as well as to the stockmen. Early in July, Indians swooped down on Buchanan Brothers' ranch on the Moccasin range, plundered the cabins, taking three Winchester rifles, two hundred rounds of ammunition, three saddles, some clothing and all the provisions in the cabin and drove off eleven head of horses. Before going they cut up two sets of harness that they found hanging in the cabin, and strewed the pieces all about the corral. They also left two horses that they had stolen from a ranch in Judith basin and ridden so hard and abused so unmercifully that one died and the other was rendered worthless.

The Buchanans discovered their loss when they re-turned home after an absence of two days. Buchanan rode thirty miles to Fort Maginnis and reported his losses to the commander, which required one day. The commander telegraphed to his superior officer, stationed at Fort Benton. He telegraphed to the commander of the division of Montana at Fort Shaw and he to the commander of the Department of the Missouri at Fort Snelling, Minnesota. By the same roundabout way the order came to send a detachment of cavalry from Fort Maginnis after the Indians. The order was received just eight days after the cabin had been plundered and the horses driven away.

Where were the Indians? The troops had no way of telling even the direction they had taken. A small detachment in command of a lieutenant started out in a northeasterly direction. I suppose they chose that course because it was straight out from the road leading from the parade ground. By some happy, or rather unhappy chance, this little body of soldiers ran into a Crow raiding party camped near Haystack buttes, about thirty miles from the fort. There were fourteen Indians in the party with sixty head of stolen horses. The Indians were taken completely by surprise, as they had not expected to encounter soldiers in that out of the way place. The Indians were placed under military escort and the party, together with the stolen horses, headed for Fort Maginnis. Eleven of the Indians riding eleven of the best horses made their escape, the three remaining Indians and the horses arrived at the fort.

These Indians were not the ones that had plundered the Buchanan ranch but they had come up from the Crow agency south of the Yellowstone, crossed the Musselshell west of the big bend, passed around the Little Snowies through the Judith basin and were heading for the mouth of the Musselshell, stealing horses along the route.

I, in company with one of our stock detectives, went to the fort, inspected the horses and found we could identify every brand and that the horses belonged mostly to small ranchers. I proposed to Colonel Smith, commander at Fort Maginnis, that he turn the horses over to me, I would put them in pasture and notify the owners that the horses were at our ranch.

Colonel Smith agreed to this plan and I sent notices to the owners of the horses, when a telegram arrived from General Terry, commanding the Department of the Missouri, stationed at Fort Snelling, Minnesota, ordering the horses and the three Indians sent to the Crow agency to be turned over to the Indian agent at that place. The owners of the horses, all poor men, began to arrive at the ranch, some having come a distance of one hundred and twenty-five miles only to learn that their horses were on the way to the Crow reservation under military escort. These people never did recover their property.

Shortly after this occurrence, a war party of twenty-two Crow Indians left their reservation with the avowed intention of stealing horses: and they left with the knowledge and consent of their agent. This same agent knew that his wards would have to cross two hundred miles of country, partially settled and occupied by white people, and that while on this raid they would necessarily have to live off of the white men's cattle, and that when stealing and plundering, Indians do not discriminate between white or Indian enemies. They take anything at hand. As soon as these Indians were off their reservation they separated into groups of five or six Indians each and scattered, some going north and east as far as the mouth of the Yellowstone and others into the Judith basin and north to the Missouri.

One of these parties, with thirty stolen horses, was captured fourteen miles north of the fort and brought in. About the time the Indians and horses arrived at Fort Maginnis; Charles L. Bristol of Dupuyn and William Cantrell, one of our stock detectives, came to the ranch. They were in pursuit of the Indians who had stolen eighteen head of horses from Bristol. When they learned that five Indians and thirty horses had just been brought into the fort, they, in company with Reece Anderson, from our ranch, went to the fort, stated their loss to Colonel Forsythe and asked to see the stolen horses.

Colonel Forsythe not only refused to allow them to see the horses, but was rude and insulting in his remarks, insinuating by both his word and action that they wished to look at the horses for the purpose of taking their description so as to give it to confederates who could then come and claim the horses with intent to dishonestly obtain possession of them.

Charles L. Bristol was a rancher, well-known and had his brands recorded. William Cantrell was a territorial officer and Reece Anderson was a rancher living three miles from Fort Maginnis with cattle and horses on the range and his brands duly recorded, so there could not be the slightest chance of either of the three gentlemen laying claim to any property that did not belong to them or would they have confederates who would do so. The three men returned to the ranch and the only explanation for Colonel Forsythe's conduct seemed to be, that he was considerably under the influence of liquor at the time of the interview.

In the morning I drove up to the fort and asked permission to examine the brands on the horses in order that I could state to the commanding officer who the owners were, so that he could turn the horses over to them. At this interview, Colonel Forsythe was sober but treated me with scant courtesy and refused to allow me to see the horses. Later, Colonel Forsythe, in reporting the occurrence to his superior officer, Colonel

Brooks, said that he refused to allow us to see the stolen animals as he wished to turn them over to the sheriff of the county.

Next morning we stood at our gate with Mr. Bristol and watched the five Indians mounted on five of the best of the stolen horses; escorted by a company of cavalry; drive the remaining twenty-three poor, tired, footsore, skinned-backed beasts, past us on their way to Fort Custer, one hundred and fifty miles further from the place where they had been stolen.

Eighteen of the thirty stolen horses were shot and left by the roadside because they became exhausted and could not stand the pace kept by the grain-fed, well-cared-for cavalry horses. There was no occasion for killing the poor beasts, because they were only suffering from over-driving and the abuse they received at the hands of the Indians. Had they just left them beside the road there was plenty of water and grass and they would soon have recovered.

These Indians were safely conducted to their reservation, turned loose without the slightest punishment and what became of the rest of the stolen horses we never learned.

The stockmen, through their association, asked for an explanation by what authority Colonel Forsythe or any other officer, authorized and allowed his soldiers to shoot exhausted horses that had been stolen and were being driven wilfully and knowingly directly away from their owners. A satisfactory explanation was never given.

These experiences of the citizens of Montana proved that it was harder to recover their property from the military than it was from the original Indian thieves.

This action was direct encouragement to the raiders. They had all the fun of stealing the horses and were then safely escorted through the danger zone to their reservation and turned loose, there to be a "big gun" in the tribe.

There was nothing left for the stockmen and ranchers to do but to deal with the Indian thieves as we had dealt with the white ones. If Indians came on the range they did so at their peril and there would be no more military parades across the country, in which our horses would figure prominently if we could help it.

Two weeks later a party of Crow Indians, presumably some of the same outfit that left their reservation with permission to prey upon the Piegans, appeared on the head of Armell's creek and drove off a band of young stock horses. The horses were not missed for several days but we had reason to believe that the Indians were still lurking about: so a small party from the ranch went after them. We found the trail and followed hard after them.

In the bad lands of the Missouri the Indians dropped the horses and scattered and so made their escape, and I presume eventually reached the shelter of their reservation in safety but they did not get any horses and they did not ride in state across the range with a military escort. In August a party of Piegans crossed the Missouri river at the mouth of the Musselshell and went on a raid of retaliation down into the Crow country. On their way home they crossed the Yellowstone at the mouth of Clark's fork and started north, keeping west of the Crazy mountains and east of the Belt range. On Smith's river they began to steal horses from the ranchers on the Highwoods and Shonkin ranges.

Everybody was haying and they made a point of gathering in the horses from the hay ranches which was particularly hard on the ranchers.

A party from the Shonkin range started in pursuit and we were notified that the Indians were headed in our direction and would likely come onto our range. We knew that in all probability they would try to cross the Missouri river at their favorite crossing, the mouth of Arrow creek. Our stock detective took two men and started out hoping to intercept them at the crossing or to overtake them before they could reach their reservation.

A company of cavalry was camped on Arrow creek near the mouth. There had been no Indians about and the soldiers were lounging in camp, taking things easy, when the Indians came over a low range of hills and were fairly in the soldiers' camp before they were aware of the presence of troops or before the soldiers suspected the presence of Indians. The surprise was mutual and complete, and before the soldiers recovered the Indians made their escape, but they were obliged to leave the horses, sixty head in all.

The soldiers rounded up the horses and started with them for Fort Maginnis. Ten miles from the fort, William Cantrell, our stock detective, and two men from the ranch met the soldiers bringing the horses in and turned and helped drive them. This enabled them to examine the brands and the horses.

Early next morning the party from the Shonkin range and Smith river arrived and went with the stock detectives to the fort to claim their horses, but were not allowed to see them. They then demanded that the horses be turned over to the two stock detectives, but were informed that the horses would be sent to the Crow agency and that they could put in their claims at that place. We told the commander that the thieves were not Crow Indians but Piegans and gave him proof to substantiate our statement but to this he paid not the slightest attention.

Several days later a detachment of soldiers, under command of a lieutenant, came down the road on their way to the Crow agency with the horses. As soon as the little cavalcade passed the ranch, William Cantrell, our stock detective, with two cow boys, intercepted them and demanded of the lieutenant that the horses be turned over to him. At first there was some hesitancy, but one look along the barrel of Cantrell's rifle and at the set determined face of the man behind the gun, decided the question and the lieutenant and his little command returned to the fort leaving the horses with Cantrell, all of which, but ten, belonged to white men. Six were Crow Indians' ponies and four belonged to the Piegans. The six belonging to the Crows were turned over to their agent. The four belonging to the Piegan thieves were sold and the money used to help defray expenses of recapturing the horses and the remaining fifty were returned to their owners. This was the last attempt of the military to hold horses, stolen from white men by the Indians.

From this time on, bands of roving Indians found on the range with or without permits from their agents, were promptly escorted to their reservations and warned never to come on the range again. Those caught in the act of stealing horses or killing cattle, or with the stolen property in their possession were punished just as the white thieves had been.

These methods together with the assistance of some very efficient sheriffs of the "range counties" and of our stock detectives enabled us to control the situation fairly well: but the cause of the evil which was the large reservations and our Indian policy, still remained an injustice and an injury to both the Indian and the white settlers.

In the territory of Montana, fifty-eight hundred square miles of land were set apart as Indian reservations, allowing more than three thousand acres of land to every man, woman, and child in the tribes for whom they were set aside: and of which they made no use other than as breeding grounds for a race of permanent and prolific paupers. The only mark of civilization on these immense reservations was the agency where resided the Indian agent and his few assistants. It permitted the Indians to choose isolated places where they collected in large numbers under their chief and so fostered and perpetuated their race prejudices, shiftless idleness, and vicious propensities. It kept them from the only civilizing influences possible to them; contact and intercommunication with the white settlers.

The greater portion of their lands extended along the international boundary between the United States and Canada and as the Indians were all one blood and spoke the same language, it was impossible to keep them from visiting back and forth. On these trips they stole horses and killed cattle and could not be punished because they could not be caught.

These border reservations further afforded a safe asylum for whiskey degenerate specimens of the white race, who gained residence on the reservation through marriage with the women of the tribes and by such association transmitted to the Indians their diseases and vices.

The Indian agent did not take trips of hundreds of miles over these reservations to see what was going on, and it would have done him no good if he had, for the Indians would not have informed on one another or on the white man who through marriage had become one of the tribe. The Indians usually distrusted their agent and kept as far away from the agency as possible, only going there to draw rations or annuities.

Although these Indians never had any responsible form of government they were recognized as free and independent nations, and the United States paid tribute to them in the way of appropriations to support them in vicious idleness. They were allowed to go fully armed with the latest improved repeating rifles, mounted on good horses, and given *carte blanche* to steal. When they were in danger of falling into the hands of the territorial officials and of losing their loot, they were taken under the wing of the military and triumphantly conducted to the safe shelter of their reservation.

In this environment they learned the white man's vices and forgot the red man's virtues and from almost physically perfect, self-respecting savages, they degenerated into a hoard of renegade pauper vagabonds. This was through no fault of their own. White men placed upon a reservation, armed, mounted, and isolated, and supported in idleness by the government would speedily degenerate into pauper robbers, for like the Indian they would lack the motive for honorable exertion.

In an endeavor to remedy this deplorable condition

I brought the matter before the National Stock Growers' Association at its meeting in Chicago in November, 1885, by introducing resolutions outlining a plan of procedure that would put a stop to Indian depredations and at the same time would be just to the Indians.

The following plan was recommended and endorsed by the delegates from thirty-two states and territories.

Disarm and dismount the Indians. Give them land in severalty with title inalienable for fifty years. Sell all of their surplus land to actual settlers, thus intermixing them with the whites, where they would learn to be self-supporting in a single generation by force of example, contact, and stern necessity.

From the sale of lands create a fund to start them in life and to aid them for a few years. Reduce them from being foreign nations to the level of all other citizens.

Protect them fully in all their rights of person and property and punish them for their crimes precisely as all other citizens are protected and punished.

Had this been done it would have solved the much vexed Indian question and from ignorant pauper thieves they would in time become self-supporting American citizens, for they lack neither brains nor muscle if compelled to use them.

End of the Cattle Range

During the summer of 1885 more than one hundred thousand head of cattle were brought into Montana, most of them trailed up from the South. There were also many bands of sheep driven in and these together with the natural rapid increase (under the most favorable conditions) trebled the number of sheep in the territory and by the fall of 1885 the Montana ranges were crowded. A hard winter or a dry summer would certainly bring disaster. There was no way of preventing the over-stocking of the ranges as they were free to all and men felt disposed to take big chances for the hope of large returns. The range business was no longer a reasonably safe business; it was from this time on a "gamble" with the trump cards in the hands of the elements.

During the summer we kept our beef cattle in the grassy cañons and along the rolling foothills at the base of the mountains. In these favored places the grass was good and water plentiful and the cattle did not lose flesh traveling long distances to water as they did when left down in the plains.

These cañons were very beautiful and there were many lovely wild flowers growing here that I had not found anywhere else in Montana. There were tiger lillies, Maraposa lillies, white purple clematis, laurel, several varieties of the orchid family, wild primroses, the Scotch bluebells, several varieties of larkspurs and lobelia, and the most fragrant and beautiful wild roses that I had ever seen. There were also choke-cherries, huckleberries, wild raspberries, and gooseberries.

The autumn foliage was beautiful; groves of golden quaking aspen, orange cottonwood, scarlet thorn-bushes, crimson rose briers, and the trailing clematis with its white cotton balls intermingling with the ever-green of the pines, fir, and spruce.

In the fall we had two thousand head of beef cattle ready for shipment when a great rush of half fat range stuff from Texas, Indian Territory, and New Mexico flooded the markets and the price of beef cattle fell to a low water-mark. We cut out all of our three year old steers and turned them back on the range and only shipped nine hundred and eighty-two head. This left us eighteen thousand eight hundred and eighty head of stock on the range after the fall shipment.

This year the National Cattle Growers' Association met in Chicago on November 17-18. The Montana delegation devoted their time and energies to two subjects, namely:

To have the government perfect and take charge of a system of quarantine against diseases of animals in all the states and territories; and to have the Indians allotted their lands in severalty and the rest of their immense reservations thrown open to actual settlers. We succeeded in having our resolutions adopted and a delegation appointed to take them to Washington and have them presented before Congress.

There was a big fight led by the delegations from Texas and Indian territory, to set aside a wide strip of country from Texas to the British line for a cattle trail and to allow the leasing from the government of the public domain. These measures did not pass.

I returned from Chicago to the range late in December accompanied by the Marquis De Mores and we stopped off at Glendive and hunted for a week. The country was dry and dusty with only an occasional snow drift in the coulees and in deep ravines. The Marquis was anxious to visit Butte, our then flourishing mining town, and as I was going there on business he continued on with me to Helena and then to Butte.

In 1885, Butte was a hustling, bustling, mining town and everything ran wide open. We arrived at seven o'clock in the evening on a little local stub from Garrison. Volumes of yellowish sulphuric smoke rolled up from the heaps of copper ore that was roasting on the flat east of Meaderville and spread over the town like a pall enveloping everything in midnight darkness and almost suffocating one. The depot was little better than a box car and the light from the windows did not penetrate the darkness. We could not see and we could scarcely breathe.

The Marquis grabbed my arm and between sneezes gasped – "What is this to which you have brought me?"

As the cab slowly crawled along the street, music from the saloons and dance halls floated out to us but we could not even see the lights in the windows. Next day it was no better and I began to feel that our visit to Butte was destined to be a disappointment in so far as seeing the town was concerned. About ten o'clock a stiff breeze blew up from the south and scattered the smoke and we were able to visit our friends, transact business, and then view the novel sights of a big mining camp.

At the meeting of the Stock Growers' Association at

Miles City, Dr. Azel Ames, F. C. Robertson, Marquis De Mores and myself were appointed a committee to confer with the people of St. Paul for the purpose of inducing them to establish stockyards and a cattle market at that city so as to relieve us from the monopoly held over us by Chicago. We succeeded in our mission and the following autumn the St. Paul yards were ready to receive shipments of cattle.

This spring we lost quite a number of cattle from their eating poisonous plants. It was the first trouble of the kind that we had encountered. These poisonous plants made their appearance after the drouths and when the grass was eaten out. Being drouth resisting they come up early, grow luxuriantly and are the first green things to appear in the spring and the cattle will eat them.

The spring roundup did not start until May 25, because with the continued drouth the green grass would not start. The cattle were in fine condition and the "calf crop" unusually large. Our outfit branded thirty-eight hundred and eighty-one calves on this roundup.

At this time a group of eastern capitalists offered to purchase our entire herd. Negotiations reached the point where we were to turn the outfit over to them, when Mr. Elkins, the man who represented the eastern company, died suddenly and the sale was not consummated.

The drouth continued and in July the short grass was dry and parched, streams and water holes drying up; but in spite of the drouth and short grass, cattle were being brought in from Washington and Oregon and the herds from the south were coming in undiminishing numbers and they were all thrown on the already over-stocked ranges of Montana.

Added to the drouth was unprecedented heat. The thermometer stood at one hundred to one hundred and ten degrees in the shade for days at a time and then would come hot winds that licked up every drop of moisture and shriveled the grass. There was nothing to be done but move at least a part of the herd.

In July I started out to look for better range and after going through the lower Judith basin, Shonkin, Highwoods, Belt creek, Sun river, and Teton ranges, finally decided to drive some of the cattle north of the Missouri river, along the foot of the Little Rockies. There was more water over there and some good grass.

In spite of every precaution range fires would start and as it was so hot and dry it was very hard to put them out when they did start. Big fires along the foot of the Judith range and on the Musselshell filled the air with smoke and cinders. Crews of fire fighters were kept busy all summer.

On arriving home, I found a telegram from Conrad Kohrs stating that he had leased range in Canada and to prepare to move. He failed to state where the leased range was located. I was not in favor of taking the herd north of the British line because of the severe blizzards that swept the open treeless plains that afforded no shelter for stock and was too far north to get the warm chinook winds. It was too late in the season to move the cattle a great distance. It always injures range cattle more or less to move them and it would never do to throw them on a strange range too late in the season.

A meeting of the stockholders of the Pioneer Cattle Company decided that we would reduce the herd as much as possible by shipping to market all the cattle fit for beef, gather the bulls and feed them at the home ranches and move five thousand head across the Missouri river to the foot of the Little Rockies. To G. P. Burnett was given the difficult task of gathering and moving the herd.

The beef could not be shipped until fall so the fat steers must not be disturbed and it was very hard to drive out the others and not disturb them, for all were as wild as antelope. Extreme care had to be used so that the herd would reach the new range in as good condition as possible.

August 10 we began gathering the cattle that were to be moved. Ordinarily one could see for miles across the range in our clear atmosphere, but not so at this time. Dense smoke obscured everything and this together with the cinders and the clouds of hot dry alkali dust almost choked and blinded us, causing much suffering to men and horses.

Moving a mixed herd is always hard. The young cattle travel fast and the old cows and young calves go slowly, so the whole herd has to be driven to suit the pace of the slowest animal in it. The drive to the new range was not a long one but under the existing circumstances it was a hard one and taxed to the fullest the ingenuity of the plucky young Texan in charge of the herd.

The weather continued extremely hot, and creeks, water-holes, and small lakes, never before dry, were completely so now. The water in all the flowing streams was very low and strongly alkaline, so much so, that in places the tired and thirsty horses refused to drink. It was so bitter that one could not drink the coffee made with it. Nearly every man with the drive was ill from drinking it. For days the herd moved forward through the smoke and stifling dust across the dry parched country.

At last we were nearing the Missouri river, intending to cross at Rocky Point. The wind was from the north and the cattle smelled the water and broke for it. No power on earth could stop the poor thirsty beasts; bellowing and lowing they ran pell-mell for the water, with the cowboys in hot pursuit. There was a point of quicksand in the river just above the ford and before the men could prevent it the cattle had plunged into it and were miring down. A small steamboat tied at the landing used their donkey engine to help drag out some of them, but we lost seventy head in spite of our best efforts.

After this mishap we crossed the herd without further trouble and from here on there was more water and better grass. The herd reached its destination in splendid condition. This fall we branded two thousand and seventy-four calves.

Seven thousand head of cattle belonging to the Powder River Cattle Company crossed the Missouri river at Great Falls and were driven through the Judith basin destined for our range, but when they saw the condition of the range and found that we were moving cattle out, they continued on north across the British line and threw their herds on the range near Fort McLeod.

John H. Conrad also had two thousand seven hundred head that he intended to bring in, but later drove them north of the line to the Cypress hills.

These changes, together with the very heavy shipments of beef to the markets relieved the over-stocked condition of the range and could we have had copious

rains early in the fall to start the grass and a reasonably easy winter, all would have gone well.

We did not get the fall rains. There was quite a
severe storm in November. On the sixteenth the
thermometer fell to two degrees below zero, with a
cutting northeast wind and on the seventeenth and
eighteenth six inches of snow fell, but blew into drifts.
The cattle north of the Missouri being unaccustomed
to the range drifted badly and kept working back to the
river.

This year we noticed that the wild animals moved
south. The wild geese and ducks and song birds
started south early and many that were accustomed to
stay with us all winter disappeared: even the range
cattle seemed to take on a heavier, shaggier coat of hair.
For the first time since I had come to the range, the
white Arctic owls came on the range and into the
Judith basin. The old Indians pointed to them and
drawing their blankets more closely about them, gave a
shrug and "Ugh! Heap Cold!" expressive of some
terrible experience in the long past that still lingered
in their memory. One old Gros Ventre warrior as-
sured me that not since he was a small boy had he seen
the owls on their reservation. Everything pointed to a
severe winter and we made what preparations we could
to meet it with as little suffering to the stock and loss
to ourselves as possible.

December 5, there was another storm, with the thermometer twelve degrees below and four inches of snow.
I returned home from Chicago December 14 and rode
from Custer station to the ranch, distant one hundred
and twenty miles, in a blizzard, the thermometer down
to zero and high east wind that pierced to the marrow
of my bones.

Between the Musselshell and Flat Willow the snow blew in our faces so that the driver could not keep the road. There were two other passengers on the stage besides myself and we took turns walking ahead of the horses with a lantern to guide them. This storm lasted three days and then cleared up warm and bright and remained so until January 9, 1887. On that day a cold wind blew from the north. It began to snow and snowed steadily for sixteen hours, in which sixteen inches of snow fell on a level. The thermometer dropped to twenty-two degrees below zero, then twenty-seven degrees, then thirty degrees, and on the night of January 15 stood at forty-six degrees below zero, and there were sixteen inches of snow on the level. It was as though the Arctic regions had pushed down and enveloped us. Everything was white. Not a point of bare ground was visible in any direction. This storm lasted ten days without abating. The cattle drifted before the storm and fat young steers froze to death along their trails.

Conditions were so changed from what they were in 1880-81. The thick brush and tall rye-grass along the streams that afforded them excellent shelter at that time was now all fenced in and the poor animals drifted against those fences and perished.

Our herd was one of the first large herds brought into northeastern Montana, consequently had been on the range longer than others. They were all northern grown range stock and occupied the best range in the northwest. We kept plenty of men on the range to look after them as best they could, keeping them back from the rivers, and out of air holes and open channels in the ice, helping them out of drifts and keeping them in what shelter the cut banks and ravines offered. The herd could be said to be a favored one, yet we lost fifty per cent of them in this storm.

There was a series of storms in February and while not so severe yet they came at a time when the cattle were least able to withstand them and there were heavy losses then. The cows were all thin and the losses in spring calves was about thirty per cent.

The herds that were driven up from the south and placed on the range late in the summer, perished outright. Others lost from seventy-five to eighty per cent of their cattle.

It was impossible to tell just what the losses were for a long time as the cattle drifted so badly in the big January storm. We did not get some of ours back for a year. Our entire losses for the year were sixty-six per cent of the herd. In the fall of 1886 there were more than one million head of cattle on the Montana ranges and the losses in the "big storm" amounted to twenty million dollars. This was the death knell to the range cattle business on anything like the scale it had been run on before.

Charles Russell, "The Cow Boy Artist" told the story of the "snuffing out of the big ranges" most graphically in his charcoal sketch, "The Last of 5000." Charlie was in charge of a herd in the Judith basin, when the owner, who lived in Helena, wrote and asked how his cattle was getting along? For answer Charlie sent him the sketch.

The large outfits were the heaviest losers as they could not feed or shelter their immense herds. Most of the big outfits had borrowed large sums of money at a high rate of interest and the cattle that they had left would hardly pay their indebtedness. They had to stay in the business and begin all over again. Eastern men who had large sums of money invested, closed out the remnant of their herds and quit.

The rancher with a good body of hay land and from one hundred to two hundred head of cattle was the man that profited He had hay enough to feed through storms and could gather his cattle around the ranch and partially shelter them, and in the spring he was enabled to buy cattle cheap. Here again I wish to say a word in defense of the "cattle barons" whom our leading newspapers abused so unmercifully at the time, accusing them of driving settlers from their homes and of "hogging" all the land. There were a good many settlers who had milch cows and a few "dogies" and did not have hay enough to feed them. The big ranches all had more or less hay and could have saved a few cattle by feeding, but instead they let the man with a family and a few cows have the hay to save their domestic animals; and they did not sell it to them at ruinous prices either but let them have it at cost of production.

In the spring of 1887 the ranges presented a tragic aspect. Along the streams and in the coulees everywhere were strewn the carcasses of dead cattle. Those that were left alive were poor and ragged in appearance, weak and easily mired in the mud holes.

A business that had been fascinating to me before, suddenly became distasteful. I wanted no more of it. I never wanted to own again an animal that I could not feed and shelter.

The spring was very wet, one heavy rain followed another in succession and the grass came on luxuriantly. We moved the remainder of the herd over on the Milk river range. I did not like the country and did not move over there. Conrad Kohrs took the management of the herd.

Much has been said and written about the extravagant mismanagement of the big cow outfits, of the selfish arrogance of the cattlemen, of the wild and reckless irresponsible cow boy.

I began at the beginning and was with it to the end and I want to say that there was never a great business that was systematized and worked more economically than the range cattle business. Some of the big outfits were owned by eastern capitalists who invested for their sons, boys who were fascinated with the free untrammeled life of the west, others were owned by men who, like myself, had been more or less in cattle in Montana for years and these small herds became the nucleus for the big outfits. Then there were men like Conrad Kohrs who had never done anything but raise cattle, and there were cattle breeders (range men) from the southwest.

It was apparent from the first that to be successful the entire range business must be run as one outfit, hence the two strong organizations, The Montana Stock Growers' Association and the Board of Stock Commissioners. These two organizations acted as Boards of Directors and they ran the cattle business absolutely. Their administration was just, honest, and economical, so much so that they have been in operation for thirty-five years and are still in operation.

The young men, scions of wealthy and influential families, loved the business and were anxious to learn, and under the leadership of older and more experienced heads, developed into splendid business men, many of them still in the state and numbered among our best citizens.

The handling of the herds on the range was entrusted to the cow boys from the southwest. These men were bred and born on the range and knew how to handle range cattle. It is impossible for me to describe one of them and do him justice. Their understanding of cattle was almost supernatural, their patience, ingenuity, faithfulness, and loyalty to their outfit cannot be described. They were to their outfit what a good mother is to her family and their way of handling herds has never been improved upon.

The idea of lavish expenditure was an erroneous one. I have described the headquarters ranch of a big outfit; few rude log cabins, comprising a bunk house, a cook house, a blacksmith shop, stable and corral, with hay land enough fenced to cut a hundred tons of hay. The food provided was beans, bacon, coffee, syrup, bread and beef. A can of tomatoes or oysters was a luxury.

The big outfits never imposed on the smaller ones or on the ranchers or squatters, but helped them in every way. In fact it was the big outfits that protected the little ones and made it possible for them to settle in the uninhabited country.

The big outfits brought millions of capital into a sparsely settled country and their herds converted the millions of tons of grass that had for thousands of years gone to waste into millions of dollars worth of beef. Their heavy taxes built roads and schools and did much for the advancement of civilization.

Index

Index